GUNNER AT LARGE

GUNNER AT LARGE

The Diary of James Wood R. A.
1746–1765

Edited by
REX WHITWORTH

Foreword by
The Master Gunner, St James's Park
General Sir Thomas Morony, KCB, OBE

LEO COOPER
LONDON

First published in 1988 by
LEO COOPER
Leo Cooper is an independent imprint
of the Heinemann Group of Publishers
Michelin House, 81 Fulham Road,
London SW3 6RB
LONDON   MELBOURNE   AUCKLAND

© Rex Whitworth 1988
ISBN 0-85052-884-4

Designed by John Mitchell
Printed in England by Butler and Tanner Ltd, Frome and London

CONTENTS

ACKNOWLEDGEMENTS

Plates nos 10 and 44 are reproduced by gracious permission of Her Majesty the Queen. The editor and the publishers would also like to thank the following for permission to reproduce copyright material in this book: the Royal Artillery Institution (Nos 1, 4, 15); the National Maritime Museum (Nos 5, 26, 29, 30, 35, 42); the Trustees of the National Gallery of Scotland (No 6); the Royal Engineers Institute, Chatham (No 7); the Bibliothèque Nationale, Paris (No 8); the Bodleian Library (Nos 9, 32, 36, 38); the British Library (Nos 13a + b, 14, 16, 19a + b, 21, 22, 40); the Rotunda Museum, Woolwich (Nos 17, 18, 41); the Public Record Office (No 24); the National Library of Wales (No 23); the Black Watch Regimental Museum (No 25); the Army Museums Ogilby Trust (Nos 27a + b, 39); the Royal Artillery Mess, Woolwich (No 28); the British Library, India Office (Nos 31, 33); the National Portrait Gallery (No 37).

In compiling this book, I particularly extend my thanks to all those who have helped and encouraged me at the Royal Artillery Institution at Woolwich, for unfailing courtesy and wise advice, namely Major-General Bill Hughes, Brigadier John Lewendon, Historical Secretary, and Brigadier Teddy Ryan. Bridget Timbers, Assistant Librarian, answered all my most exacting questions and laid her hands on all the manuscripts and authorities I needed for my editorial work. I should also like to thank Colonel Pip Newton and the staff of the Army Museums Ogilby Trust. One of the Trustees, Major George Ward, late RA, saw the manuscript and was most encouraging in supporting my intention to make James Wood known to a wider public. Mr A. Stimson, Curator at The National Maritime Museum, helped to clear up navigational problems in the manuscript logs.

For typing the many drafts from the original manuscript and the various editorial passages at different times, my thanks are due to Sue Crowley, Linda Robinson and Gillian Spong.

In editing I have made considerable use of my knowledge of the Cumberland Papers at Windsor Castle and record my grateful thanks to Miss Jane Langton of the Royal Archives for much help over the years.

Finally, I should like to thank the Master Gunner at St James' Park, General Sir Thomas Morony, for saluting the work with an appropriate salvo.

Rex Whitworth
September, 1988

FOREWORD

BY THE MASTER GUNNER, ST JAMES'S PARK
GENERAL SIR THOMAS MORONY, KCB, OBE

James Wood would have been surprised that his diaries should have so much interest for us now. For him, they were simply the record of the routine existence of a junior member of the Royal Artillery serving in John Chalmers' Company. It is true that that service led him to an amphibious raid on Britanny in 1746, to operations against the French in Brabant in 1747–1748, to garrison duty in Scotland from 1749–51, and, best of all, to India in 1755, but it is plain from his diary entries that James Wood took life everywhere very much as it came. This is a factual record of events as one day succeeded another and it was maintained simply for the personal interest of James Wood.

It follows that there are few details here of the daily routine, for James Wood needed no record to remind him of that. Moreover, emotion nowhere clouds the narrative in which everything is set down simply and as a matter of fact. Even his first experiences in action are recorded drily:— "Major Bagshaw received a cannon shot in his thigh. Surgeon Butler immediately cut off his leg. . . . He is in a fair way to recovery".

For us, however, this record is by no means simple, for we in our generation are continually surprised by what were simple matters of fact in his – the use of large numbers of men to draw the guns "in men's harness" over long distances, the boredom of campaigning in those two seasons in Brabant, the remarkable manner in which John Chalmers' Company carried out its tour in Scotland by march route, and the day-to-day existence on the Coromandel coast.

Even on his way to India and facing so much that must have seemed extraordinary, James Wood refused to be astonished. For instance, having arrived in Madagascar, he found the inhabitants to be "a savage kind of people . . . . very civil to the English". Moreover, although "the most pernicious animals are crocodiles and great serpents . . . . I do not hear of any harm they do".

Of course it is in this very lack of embellishment that much of the historical value of these diaries lies. But the more general reader, too, will find a fascination in what I can only call the matter of factuality of the entries. For myself, I have much enjoyed meeting the young James Wood and have no doubt that others too will enjoy making his acquaintance. We should all be grateful to Rex Whitworth for his admirable book.

INTRODUCTION

ONLY A PORTION of Wood's original manuscript diary was left to the Royal Artillery Institution by Mrs Beatrice Lowe in 1946. Previously it appears that the complete manuscript in Wood's hand covering the years 1746 to 1765 with a gap between 1751 and 1755 was part of the collection of Royal Artillery items assembled by Mrs Lowe's father-in-law, Major Francis Manley Lowe R A, in the early part of this century. He evidently had antiquarian tastes and at the relevant time was an artillery advisor at the Armstrong Whitworth works at Elswick. While there, he typed the first section of the diary in 1912 and made some notes about the Wood family which he traced to Fulbourne in Cambridgeshire. At one time the complete diary was lent to a well-known gunner historian, Lieutenant-Colonel J.H. Leslie, to edit. A part of the diary was apparently lost at his London club on 4 July, 1941 – a war casualty. Part of the diary was also borrowed by Sir Patrick Cadell, historian of the Bombay Army.

The late Lieutenant-Colonel M.E.S. Laws transcribed as much of the diary as he could find some time after 1946 and in 1951 wrote two articles on it in the *Royal Artillery Journal*. The existing manuscript volume of the diary does not cover the period of Wood's service in India after 1760. For this period only Colonel Laws' abbreviated transcript exists but it fully covers material of army interest. For all the vicissitudes Wood's manuscript has suffered we still have a most valuable military document. It covers a very wide spectrum of military life in war and peace at a very early period of the Royal Regiment's existence and the account given of service by regular gunners in India between 1755 and 1765 is unique.

James Wood entered the Academy at Woolwich on the nomination of the Duke of Montagu, Master General of the Ordnance, in 1745. A visit to Woolwich in 1744 by the Duke of Cumberland had resulted in steps being taken to reform the discipline and system of training of the cadets. It was not, however, until 1951 that artillery officers received the King's commission like cavalry and infantry officers but the controversial system of purchase was never introduced. As a result children were not found in charge of artillery detachments and promotion for career officers could be extremely slow, as it appears to have been in Wood's case.

For his first few years of service Mattross[1] Wood served as a volunteer, only being mustered as a cadet gunner in 1754 on the eve of his going to India. His several years of active service life before this took him to Brittany in 1746, Brabant in 1747–8 and peacetime garrison duty in Perth, Scotland 1749–51. Throughout this period he served in John Chalmers' company (from which in 1965 it was agreed that 3 Light Battery R A drew its origins). He may well have had some personal association with Chalmers to be so long a volunteer with his company, and it was to be John Chalmers, as a Major in 1755, who took three companies, Royal Artillery, to Bombay. During the following continuous ten years of service in India nearly all Wood's brother officers died. Chalmers himself died in 1759. We must count ourselves extremely fortunate that our diarist survived such a remarkable variety of service. His diary bears all the marks of being a daily journal written down at the time as a record of the bare facts of service, with only a few later revisions.

When Wood returned to England in 1765 he was disquieted to find that seventeen officers junior to him had been promoted over his head. It was only in January, 1771, that he was promoted Captain/Lieutenant. After holding his brevet for seven years he became a substantive Captain in 1779. In that crisis year for home defence in the face of the Franco-Spanish Armada he was given command of a Company encamped at Warley in Essex. During the War of American Independence he served also at Woolwich, Yarmouth and Portsmouth. In March, 1783, he was promoted brevet Major and handed over his company on promotion to the technical appointment of Chief Firemaster at the Royal Laboratory at Woolwich. He was the author of several useful inventions in the field of equipment design before dying at Woolwich on 20 February, 1797, Fifty-two years after joining the Academy. Nothing after 1765 was added to his diary.

Wood's career was by no means distinguished but it was certainly useful to his Regiment. His origins appear to have been humble. He had no powerful patrons with social or political clout to further his

---

1 Mattross – the most junior rank in the artillery, below that of Gunner. He received 1/- a day, a Gunner 1/4^d.

career but as an artillery officer he had a mind trained to observe and record detail accurately and with brevity. It is this quality that makes his diary of such particular interest militarily. Representing a specialist arm, he obviously knew what went on from the angle of someone close to Headquarters and he covers general operations from a particular vantage point denied the junior officer in a marching regiment.

To build a narrative around verbatim extracts from the diary, I have divided the original material into a number of sections arranged chronologically around a specific theme, linking them in a series of short editorial interruptions. I have modernized the text as far as spelling is concerned and eliminated most of the elisions and abbreviations that hinder fluency in reading. As a consequence of the linking narrative I have reduced footnotes to a minimum. On the other hand, where it is in my view necessary to a proper understanding of military operations in the days of sail, I have left in much material concerning the navigation of convoys, which readers interested in maritime history may find informative.

I must record my thanks to the Master Gunner of St James's Park and the Royal Artillery Institution for allowing me to make use of the Wood Diary in this form. I believe it has considerable significance for the history of the army in a period too little noticed and in particular throws new light on our soldiers and sailors during the period of the most successful war we ever fought – between 1756 and 1763. We balanced a land and maritime strategy in most effective fashion. There was a great number of able officers commanding troops and crews who displayed remarkable fighting qualities all over the world, making use of equipments which proved more effective than those of their opponents. In particular the narrative covers operations on the Coromandel coast of India in addition to the more familiar Carnatic. Wood's diary gives a new insight into the skilful endeavours of our forefathers from the humble level of a junior officer of considerable intelligence and undeniable modesty.

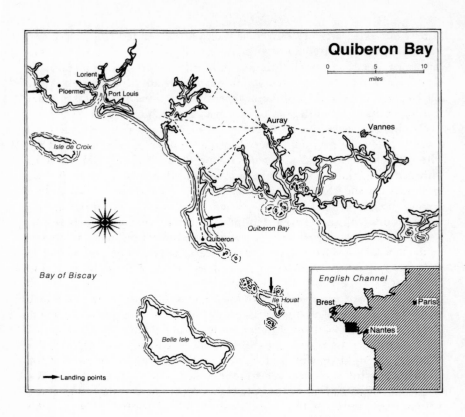

Quiberon Bay

miles

Lorient
Ploermel
Port Louis
Isle de Croix
Auray
Vannes
Quiberon Bay
Quiberon
Bay of Biscay
Ile Houat
Belle Isle
English Channel
Brest
Paris
Nantes
Landing points

A SECRET EXPEDITION

THE ORIGINS of the despatch of an amphibious raid against
France in the year of Culloden are confusing. A maritime war between
Spain and England – Jenkins' Ear – that had begun in 1739 had become
entangled in a wider struggle emanating from the dynastic rivalry
between Hapsburg and Bourbon in central Europe. The death of an
Emperor of Germany without a male Hapsburg heir in 1740 provided
the occasion for an ambitious French intervention in German affairs,
for an Italian-born queen of Spain to covet Hapsburg territories in
North Italy for her second son and for a young king of Prussia to seek
to expand his narrow kingdom, all at the expense of the 23-year-old
Maria Teresa. She was vulnerable, too, to French pressure in the
Austrian Netherlands which were ruled by her Viceroy in Brussels and
protected under treaty by a chain of Dutch garrisons in the border
towns. The commitment of Hanoverian England to the cause of Maria
Teresa in however limited a fashion was sufficient to tempt the French
ministry into mounting an expedition against London in 1744 and, on
its failure, to give a half-hearted approval to the forlorn hope of the
'45. Such acts of dynastic hostility obliged France to declare outright
war on George II. In all this, the position of the Protestant Estates of
republican Holland was somewhat equivocal, though mutual arrange-
ments had allowed George II to advance to the help of Austria through
Dutch territory in 1743 and required the Dutch to send regiments over
to Newcastle in 1745. A small Dutch field force had fought ineffectually
beside the British against Marshal Saxe at Fontenoy in 1745 under the
command of William, Duke of Cumberland, Captain General of the
British Army. Yet for all this by 1746 Holland was still not a full
belligerent against France, and the merchants of Amsterdam, the then
financial centre of Europe, were by no means bellicose. They were more
particularly wary since the unexpected success of the Young Pretender
in 1745 had caused the withdrawal of Cumberland and most of the

British and Hessian troops. This led to the capture by France during the winter of 1745/46 of both Brussels and Antwerp, placing armies upon the very frontier of Holland itself.

Across the oceans the Anglo-French quarrel was carried on more directly and energetically than in Europe. In North America the British colonists from New England had successfully combined with a squadron of the Royal Navy in 1745 to seize the main French North Atlantic base at Louisburg on Cape Breton Island. Thus the St Lawrence lay open for British sea power to exploit in the summer days of 1746 as far as Quebec and the French feverishly sought to build up at Brest a squadron strong enough to take revenge by the seizure of Halifax, Nova Scotia. Far away in India the forces of the rival East India companies struggled for hegemony in the Carnatic but with considerably less direction from Paris than from London.

The Duke of Bedford at the Admiralty longed to exploit French weakness in Canada but the Duke of Cumberland looked to a return to Flanders with his victorious regiments from Culloden. However, he was delayed in Scotland harrying the highlands and then his father would not let him go, preferring rather to sustain Maria Teresa and the Dutch by sending a few battalions under Sir John Ligonier to serve under Austrian command along the middle Meuse. This allowed for a force of six battalions to be convoyed across the Atlantic in time to sail up the St Lawrence that summer. In early April, 1746, colonial governors in America were asked to raise levies to join in the attack with the British expedition which it was hoped to get away in May. The commander appointed was General James Sinclair, the second son of Lord Sinclair, and Colonel of the Royal Scots, the 1st of Foot. (His elder brother had been out in the '15 and attainted). No admiral was appointed until a court martial had acquitted the elderly Charles Lestock on a charge of failing to support Admiral Matthews, his commander-in-chief, in an action against the French off Toulon eighteen months before. Having pleaded successfully the technicalities of the Fighting Instructions to explain his lack of enthusiasm for the fight, he was immediately promoted Vice Admiral on acquittal and put in charge of the expedition against Quebec. He used considerable vigour and administrative know-how to collect up a squadron of clean ships and full crews to man them, much to the irritation of Admiral Anson, who was in the process of taking over the Channel fleet. To maintain two fully crewed and seaworthy fleets in the circumstances of 1746 was a tall order. By the time Anson was ready for sea not only had Admiral the Duc D'Enville slipped out of Brest with his avenging fleet but the year was too far gone for Lestock and Sinclair to hope to do more than reach Boston. It was at this juncture, in August, that the Secretary of State, the Duke of Newcastle, became doubtful of the strength of Dutch resolution in the face of a determined diplomatic French peace offensive. He despatched the young Lord Sandwich to observe the Franco-Dutch talks at Breda and believed he could best hold the Dutch to their allegiance by promising a seaborne attack on the French mainland. This, he assured them through Sandwich, would cause the French to divert forces from the Dutch frontier.

Certainly George II was not particularly interested in North America, and Cumberland, though preferring greater deployment into Holland direct, was not against reinforcing a successful landing on the French coast with a Guards Brigade, should Newcastle's wild scheme succeed. Neither Sinclair nor Lestock was particularly taken with Newcastle's proposal, which required them to make suggestions for a raid anywhere from the Gironde to Normandy. They were nervous of venturing into the Bay of Biscay in the autumn and jumped at the suggestion of Normandy. But this was not favoured by the King or Newcastle. It was only finally in September, at Plymouth, whither the escorting fleet and transports had drifted slowly during the summer, that the precise objective was agreed on. It was probably on Anson's advice that Sinclair and Lestock decided to have a go at the French East India Company's base at L'Orient in Brittany, three miles up the River Bavet. Surrounded by unsubstantial town walls it was full of warehouses. There was a good chance to burn some shipping too.

General Sinclair's Secretary was the distinguished philosopher and historian, David Hume, and we are fortunate indeed to have the comments of his remarkable mind on the fumblings of the military machine. There was no intelligence available on L'Orient and the only map that he could procure from a shop in Plymouth was a small-scale one of the whole of France. Lestock wisely sent forward Commodore Coats in HMS *Ruby* to reconnoitre the coast and two days later on 1st September (New Style) the main fleet reached for Quimperlé Bay. Nine men of war – Lestock in HMS *Princessa*, a captured Spanish prize, two sloops, a fire ship, the *Mortar* bomb ketch with a detachment of Royal Artillery – escorted thirty-three transports carrying six regiments, of which three, the Royals, Lord John Murray's (42nd Highlanders), and Braggs' (28th Foot), had fought at Fontenoy. Detachments of three marine regiments, Captain John Chalmers' company of Royal Artillery with young James Wood, and three other infantry battalions, Harrison's (15th Foot), Frampton's (30th) and Richbell's (39th), whom James Wood would meet again in India, brought the force up to about 4000 men. No cavalry were shipped and no horses or wagons for the artillery train, though L'Orient was some nine miles overland by indifferent tracks from the landing place. Three companies of Frampton's seem actually to have been sent to Cape Breton Island and many of the regiments were made up at the last minute at Portsmouth with drafts of deserters from the Savoy prison in London, where it was the custom to put delinquents awaiting transportation.

Some of the troops had been embarked for Quebec as early as April, but were given a run ashore at Portsmouth when rations and water ran short. Wood's artillery company remained aboard from May onwards in their seven transports hired by the Board of Ordnance at 1/- a ton a month. The commander of the artillery at General Sinclair's head-quarters was a civilian engineer by the name of Thomas Armstrong who held no army rank. He was assisted by four other engineers, including Justly Watson, who had had operational experience, Clarke, who was to lose his reputation at Rochefort in 1757, and young William Green, who was to become one of the most famous of engineer officers and the true founder of the modern corps of Royal Engineers. He was to win undying fame as Chief Engineer at the great siege of Gibraltar under Lord Heathfield in 1779–1782. It was at L'Orient that he first saw red hot shot in the form of flaming carcass bombs. Armstrong's plan was to set L'Orient and its storehouses and shipping on fire. He had no siege, only field, guns and so sanguine was he that he discouraged Sinclair from accepting an early surrender by the French. So incom-petent was he that initially he neglected to bring forward the portable furnace to heat the shot and, having got it forward, was unable to work it because the bellows had been left aboard ship.

Lestock and Sinclair achieved a surprise landing but Lestock had no wish to remain close to a lee shore in the Bay of Biscay at the latter end of September and was always urging re-embarkation. Some of Sinclair's untried infantry panicked when his left column was fired on by the French militia from a flank. The subsequent court martial proceedings at Cork give a fascinating insight into 18th century discipline. Lord John Murray presided and, despite redirection through David Hume, acting as Judge Advocates General, acquitted most of those arraigned because he considered that Sinclair had condoned their offence by not arresting or charging them at the time of their misbehaviour. The few who were found guilty and sentenced to death were all pardoned by George II because he felt the poor men had suffered enough by the time the papers reached him for confirmation.

Wood's account of this "Secret Expedition" brings out in vivid, though unvarnished detail, the extraordinary difficulties of amphibious operations in the days of sail. I have purposely left in all the detail of routine ship movements to underline these points. When General Sinclair got aboard on 12 July he was still under the impression that he was due for Quebec and, apart from the two short periods on land at L'Orient and Quiberon, remained aboard until reaching Cork in mid-November. Lestock, who is said to have had a seasick lady friend aboard, was nearly 70, full of rheumatism and a man of haughty and austere disposition. Though Councils of War were held on his flagship, which Captain John Chalmers R A attended, there is little to show, beyond his interesting and detailed scheme for forming his convoy, that he exercised much control during operations. Indeed, after re-embarking the troops from their first landing at L'Orient, a gale drove some of the transports off the coast altogether. Since masters had been given no local rendezvous for the next landing, some of them made the best of their way back to Falmouth. Unless a pilot from the Channel Islands had turned up, the landing at Quiberon would probably not have taken place. (Despite the failure in 1746 it was again chosen in 1795 for the disastrous landing made to help the French Royalists against the revolutionaries.) When finally Lestock sailed from Quiberon, after landing parties on two offshore islands, he lost control of a great part of his fleet. Admiral Anson was returning home up channel with the western squadron, having learnt of the nigh annihilation of Admiral D'Enville's fleet in a terrific storm off Newfoundland. "The 26th October," he reported to the Admiralty, "I fell in with eighteen sail of transports full of soldiers forty-five leagues to the westward of the Lizard without convoy. To secure them against the enemy's privateers I ordered the *Portland* to see them safe into Cork or Kinsale whither they were bound."

Wood's account gives no detail of the organization of his company. As a volunteer he was probably a supernumerary clerk to John Chalmers. The manpower of the company was only sufficient to fire the guns which the engineers emplaced in batteries with the help of working parties from the infantry and to man the field laboratory. Lack of horses meant that the sailors and the marines had to draw the 12-pounder guns and 10" mortar from the shore – no easy task along poor tracks in autumn rains with all the necessary ammunition supply and stores. It was here that the expedition, requiring the destruction or capture of a walled town, was hopelessly ill thought-out and mishandled, the French building up their counter-battery effort far quicker than the landing force.

The two short three-pounder guns which normally gave close support in the infantry line, and were distributed in pairs to battalions, were crewed by infantrymen under Royal Artillery supervision, and weighed $2\frac{1}{2}$ cwt. The long version was six feet in length and weighed 6 cwt. The 12-pounders had a barrel length from five feet (short) to nine feet (long, heavy) and weighed nine or thirty cwt. Their theoretical maximum range at 4° of elevation was 1400 yards. At L'Orient only four 12-pounders and a mortar were got into action while the French had at least twelve mounted behind the town walls. The total British rate of fire was about four rounds an hour, possibly because of Armstrong's predilection for red hot shot and carcass bombs which flew through the air belching fire through holes from the inflammatory filling. The battery was also badly sited in relation to the angle at which the shots hit the town wall, which he consequently failed to breach.

The normal crew of a gun was five: the NCO did the laying and observing; the "sponger" had the task of first ramming down and subsequently sponging out the bore from the muzzle end; at the back the "ventman", with his thumb in a leather thumbstall, covered the vent after firing, so that no smouldering grains of powder could be pushed out by the sponger. At the front, on the left, stood a fourth man who put in first the bagged charge which the ventman pricked to make ignition more certain and then the selected projectile which the sponger rammed down with the butt end of his staff. The fifth man at the left rear was the "firer". He put a smouldering port fire to the end of the tube in the vent which the ventman had inserted above the charge. The recoil of about 6 feet required the crew to push back the piece that distance on to its platform in the battery after each shot. It was essential that the engineers sited and constructed solid emplacements for such guns to fire effectively.

Back in the laboratory tent, which Wood mentions, the ammunition, fuses and so on were prepared. Field artillery shot had a diameter of from 3 to $4\frac{1}{4}$ inches. Case shot was just a tin case containing a number of loose bullets which scattered as the case left the muzzle. The optimum range was about 1200 yds and a 6-pounder held about 85 $1\frac{1}{2}$ ounce bullets. Grape shot, which tended to damage the bore of brass ordnance, was in the form of nine large bullets wired together; barred shot was two round shots joined together and much used against ship's rigging. Land and sea service ordnance pieces were identical except for the types of carriage so that sailors could be involved on land quite as usefully as Royal Artillery men, witness Braddock's expedition against Fort Duquesne in 1754 when he took sailors from Keppel's fleet all the way to disaster. In Wood's time the guns had no elevating screw or tangent sight. Elevation was achieved by tapping in wedges, or quoins, under the barrel. Changes for line were made by moving the bracket trail with handspikes.

The mortar was a heavy weapon to move about. The 13" sea service mortar manned on the bomb ketch by a Royal Artillery detachment had a weight of 5 tons and sent a shell of 200 lb up to 4000 yards at full charge. The 10" land service mortar weighed 10 cwt. The Royal, a $5\frac{1}{2}$" mortar, used by the Company at L'Orient on land, was a brass weapon, weighing $1\frac{1}{4}$ cwt. The Coehorn was a $4\frac{2}{3}$" light mortar. No howitzers were taken.

The French reactions to Sinclair's efforts at L'Orient and Quiberon were minimal. No regular troops were encountered or drawn down but a fairly numerous local militia eventually rallied to the town and some quite effective garrison or marine gunners were in action. The six battalions who landed were never reinforced by the Brigade of two Guards battalions and the Welch Fusiliers, which Cumberland had ordered to embark to support a successful landing. After a short cruise down the Channel from Gravesend they failed to locate Lestock's convoy and returned. Altogether, therefore, nine battalions of infantry and a company of artillery spent a long time at sea with no visible effect on French operations. They might well have influenced the French more, as well as the Dutch, had they engaged alongside their colleagues in the area of Liège, where Saxe gained the advantage over Charles of Lorraine and Ligonier at Rocoux.

Neither General Sinclair nor Vice Admiral Lestock saw any service after the "Secret Expedition" of 1746. The Vice Admiral retired and died within a few months, while Sinclair took David Hume with him on diplomatic missions to Vienna and Turin. He remained Colonel of the Royal Scots until 1762 when he died without ever assuming his father's title. Wood returned to Ireland from his baptism of fire still without any established post in the Royal Artillery.

A SECRET EXPEDITION

1746

WOOLWICH – MAY 3 1746 SATURDAY

Captain John Chalmers' Company of the Royal Artillery embarked on board seven transport ships with stores for a secret expedition viz: the *Westmoreland, Bosphorus, Boston, Landovery, Susanna* and *Sarah, Esther* and the *Neptune* all laden.

SUNDAY 4th Wind SW

The pilot came on board at 10 am sailed with pleasant weather to Gravesend. At 1 pm cast anchor.

TUESDAY 6th Wind NE

Weighed anchor and sailed, but entering the Hope the wind came to the eastward. Cast anchor in 6 fathom of water.

WEDNESDAY 7th Wind SW

The wind coming to the SSW sailed to the Nore; at 4 pm anchored and received instructions from the *Lark* man of war.

THURSDAY 8th Wind W

At noon HMS *Sheerness* with the *Hazard*[1] sloop lately retaken anchored here.

TUESDAY 13th Wind SW

The *Royal Sovereign* made a signal for all masters of merchantmen to give in their accounts of the loading, ships names and where bound.

---

[1] Captured by the Jacobites off Scotland after convoying General Cope for Aberdeen and subsequently retaken in 1746 by the Royal Navy

At 5 pm the Commodore made a signal and anchored near the *Squirrel* by the Naze.

WEDNESDAY 14th Wind NE
At 2 am unmoored; at 8 anchored the tide being done, in 8 fathom water about 4 miles to the westward of Shewbaken; at 4 weighed and worked down the Swine: at 8 anchored in 6 fathom water.

THURSDAY 15th Wind ENE
Sailed about 4 in the morning and about 9 am the *Lark* ran aground on the upper part of the Gun Fleet sand: she hung out a signal of distress and the ships sent their boats to tow her and by their assistance she got off. At 4 pm weighed and played to the eastward. At 9 anchored, the tide being done.

FRIDAY 16th Wind E
At 4 am weighed and passed the buoy of the Gun Fleet: at 10, the tide being done, came to an anchor in the King's Channel: at 4 pm weighed and at 8 anchored in 20 fathom.

SATURDAY 17th Wind ENE
Weighed at 9; saw the North Foreland and about 10 came to Ramsgate. At noon we went between the Goodwins and Brakes; at 1 pm anchored in the Downs near the South Foreland nigh the Castle; at 3 the pilot went on shore.

SUNDAY 18th Wind ENE
At 10 am hove up our anchor and went nearer to Upper Deal Church; anchored in 9 fathom.

TUESDAY 20th Wind NE
One Man of War with several coasting vessels sailed to the Westward. At 8 am our Commodore made a signal for unmooring.

WEDNESDAY 21st Wind NNE
Weighed from the Downs in Company with 28 sail under the Lark's convoy; about 9 left Deal on the right hand and about noon was abreast of Folkestone. Pleasant gales.

THURSDAY 22nd Wind EBE

Came in sight of the Isle of Wight and about noon anchored in St Helens in 6 fathoms. At 2 pm weighed and ran into Spithead. Anchored in 6 fathom, moderate gales ended.

WEDNESDAY 28th Wind SW

At 6 pm *Baltimore* anchored with a French prize and a sloop she had taken.

THURSDAY 29th Wind SSW

A French prize came from sea and ran to Portsmouth harbour.

SATURDAY 31st Wind SE

Our boat sent to the victualling office for fresh meat as did the rest of the transports.

MONDAY JUNE 2nd Wind SW

At noon the *St George* and *Prince Frederick* sailed and anchored at St Helens.

TUESDAY 10th Wind NBW

Mr Armstrong engineer and Commandant of the Artillery came on board the seven ships and mustered the artillery.

THURSDAY 12th Wind NE

At 6 am saw several ships coming from the East and in the afternoon anchored near 40 sail with two men of war. Received 6 weeks' provisions and one cask of brandy in each ship for the artillery.

SUNDAY 15th Wind NEBN

A signal for weighing and sailed by 6 am. Little wind which obliged the Captains to sent out their boats to tow the ships; at 1 pm anchored in 6 fathoms.

TUESDAY 24th Wind SSE

St Helens: at 4 am a signal for sailing; at 8 am sailed in company with 70 sail under Convoy of Commodore Coats in the *Edinburgh* 70 guns, *Devonshire* 80, *Tilbury* 60, *Superb* 70, *Hastings* 40 guns. Sailed until 4 pm when wind turned to the westward with violent thunder with wind and rain which obliged the fleet to turn back for St Helens but the wind coming to the eastward occasioned the fleet to bear away again;

at 6 pm the wind turned to the westward which caused the ships to sail back for St Helens and all came to an anchor at the extreme of the Isle of Wight in 24 fathoms at 10 pm: our anchor dragged near three leagues which obliged the Captain to let go the best bower anchor.

WEDNESDY 25th Wind SSE
At 2 am began to weigh and in weighing our stream cable was lost which the Captain supposed was cut by the rocks: the buoy and buoy rope of our best bower anchor was also lost; about 4 am the wind coming westerly obliged the fleet to sail back for St Helens and came to anchor in 7 fathoms.

FRIDAY 27th Wind WSW
Heavy squalls of wind, the sea all in a breach and foam. Captain Chalmers and Mr Vandenand, the Conductor, had just got into the boat to go on board the *Landovery* which was taken in the first squall and was obliged to sail for Portsmouth Harbour, the wind happening to set that way, and with great difficulty saved their lives.

SUNDAY 29th Wind SSW
All weighed and sailed for Spithead except three ships ordered for Cape Breton; at 4 anchored at Spithead in 6 fathom near Gilkicker: the Highlanders, Harrison's and the Royal Scots disembarked at Portsmouth.

WEDNESDAY JULY 2nd Wind SSW
A signal for unmooring at 6 am. Weighed at 7 am. The Pilot came on board and sailed out of the harbour; at 9 anchored at Spithead.

SATURDAY 5th Wind ENE
Orders for the three Regiments to embark on board the ships they came out of. Commodore Coats made a signal for all Masters to be in readiness for sea, and to follow the instructions received from him. Likewise received orders to make up on provisions for six months.

MONDAY 21st Wind SW
At 7 am the Blue Flag was hoisted on board the *Royal George* at the main top mast appointed for Admiral Lestock: was saluted by all the fleet.

Sunday 27th Wind SBW
At 4 pm the *Princessa* came out of harbour.

Monday 28th Wind SSW
The Blue Flag was hoisted at the main top mast head of the *Princessa* and the flag on board the *Royal George* was struck.

Friday August 1st
At 1 pm the Admiral fired a gun and loosed his fore top sail, and weighed anchor as did all the fleet under his charge, and sailed to St Helens, and cast anchor near the Warner buoy in 15 fathom.

Wednesday 6th
At 10 am a signal for sailing: at 7 am the Captain of our ship had gone on shore and at 11 am we laid to for our Captain and the long boat: a Lieutenant of the *Devonshire* came to know what we laid to for; when he was informed he caused us to make all the sail we could after the Fleet, without any regard to the Captain, but the wind turned westerly, which obliged the whole fleet to sail back for St Helens and cast anchor in 6 fathom – the Captain came on board.

Thursday 7th Wind SBE
At 10 am a signal for sailing: at 11 were all under sail, about 12 noon the wind came to the westward and put back for St Helens; at 5 the Admiral ran aground on St Helens Point about two miles from the Shore, but it happened to be Low water, and by the assistance of the Men of War's boats she got off at high water with the loss of breaking her rudder from the ship; the transports anchored at 6 and the *Princessa* at 9 am.

Saturday 16th Wind NE
At 5 the wind came NE and the Admiral made a signal for sailing, but the wind coming westerly, a signal for mooring again.

Thursday 21st Wind SWBS
At 5 am made a signal for unmooring but the wind coming to the south, so veered our cable out.

SATURDAY 23rd Wind ENE

At 5 am a signal to weigh and at 6 we all got under sail but the wind coming NBW bore away for St Helens and anchored in 6 fathom near St Helens point: light airs and hazy weather.

SUNDAY 24th Wind SE

At 4.30 am a signal to sail: at 5 we were all under sail: at 10 am we got clear of the point, at noon abreast of Dunose.

TUESDAY 26th Wind SWBS

Came in sight of Portland Castle belonging to Dorsetshire.

THURSDAY 28th

In the morning came in sight of the Eddystone and at 10 came in sight of Plymouth Sound: at 4 pm three Men of War joined us from Plymouth and at 8 we anchored in the sound in 8 fathom; the Admiral and all the men of war entered in Causand Bay.

SATURDAY 30th Wind SSW

This morning Admiral Anson anchored in Causand Bay.

WEDNESDAY SEPTEMBER 8th Wind WNW

Admiral Anson and nine men of war sailed from Causand Bay on a cruise.

FRIDAY 9th Wind SW

A great many transports slipped their cable and ran into Catwater; at 5.30 the *Buchanan* ran foul of a bilander[2] and had like to have been on shore; fired many guns of distress. The ships sent their long boats to get out the soldiers, and carried them on board the *Duke of Cumberland*: the wind coming NW the two ships got into Catwater; one of them lost her foremast, and the other was very much damaged.

SATURDAY 13th Wind NW

All the transports ordered to the Sound at noon; unmoored, and towed into the Sound; anchored in 6 fathom.

[2] A Dutch sailing vessel with trapezoidal mainsail.

SUNDAY 14th Wind W

At 6 am hove up our anchor and went further out; anchored in 6 fathom by St Nicholas Island: 1 mile from Plymouth Castle.

MONDAY 15th Wind NNW

A signal for sailing at 9 am. We weighed and came to sail at 1 pm. We laid to for some ships coming out of the Sound; at 8 we made sail.

WEDNESDAY 17th Wind SBE

Sailed in company of 49: left the Eddystone NNW. The Lizard bore NBW. Distance 5 leagues.

FRIDAY 19th Wind E

About 6 came in sight of the Island De Groix 3 leagues distant from the main land of France. About 2 pm the Admiral hoist up anchoring colours and anchored in Quimperlé Bay about 8 miles from Port L'Orient in Bretagne; the peasants put out flags of defiance and fired on our fleet from a battery on a rock of 2 eight pound brass guns. Returned their fire from the *Sapphire*, and a man of war sloop.

ORDERS By Richard Lestock Esq, Admiral of the Blue and Commander in Chief of His Majesty's ships and vessels employed

WHEREAS I have observed a general neglect in almost all the Masters of the transports and store ships, employed in HM service on the present expedition and being justly apprehensive that those who do not do so in time of coming to action or when it should be necessary to land HM troops where their ignorance or neglect might be attended with fatal effects:

The Captain and Commanders of HM ships and vessels under my command are therefore here required and directed upon all signals being made, not only diligently and judiciously to observe them, but also as far as in them lies, to oblige all Masters of transports, and store ships to do the same, according to the tenor expressed in the several articles as well of the sailing and fighting instructions, as all other additional signals assigned them by me for their due observation, and carefully to keep their prescribed stations, taking particular care to make both themselves and officers masters of the said signals, as they must expect to answer for the dangerous consequences that may attend such their neglect.

Signals and instructions to be observed for the regular anchoring with the transports and store ships, and for their having more conveniently all necessary and timely assistance from the squadron of H M ships and vessels under my command.

The ships of war, transports and store ships hereby directed to divide into the following divisions and the senior Captain of H M ships in each division for this service is required to take the several transports and store ships accordingly under their particular care and charge, and to give their masters orders from time to time, agreeable to such directions as they shall receive from me and for their assistance in keeping the said transports and store ships orderly and regularly together and in constant readiness for sailing the junior Captain of H M vessels and tenders mentioned in their respective Divisions are also directly to observe the directions of their senior captains.

When the signal is made for anchoring the senior Captain of H M ships in each division are for their distinction to hoist signal pendants at the foretop gallant masthead to visit the senior captain of the first Division. In order to avoid confusion each Division is to have a Pendant: a Red Pendant the first, the second a White, the senior of the Third a Blue, the senior of the fourth a Yellow Pendant, and to wear the said pendant until their respective Divisions are anchored and each division is to keep together, and for better observing such a proportional distance as the place will allow as well for the berthing the several Divisions in their proper stations the senior Captain is to take care to suffer no ships of his Division to anchor before himself.

When I would have any of the ships of war proceed to any place or harbour where I may think proper I will hoist the anchoring colours at the foretop masthead and fire 2 guns and put a broad pendant for speaking with the Captain of the ship, who is to make the best of his way together with the ships or vessels, named in the margin, appointed to attend him upon that service, to the place where the Fleet is to anchor.

Being come thither he is to observe the following method in placing the 4 signal ships for the 4 Divisions and they must wear the following marks of distinction, that for the first a Red Pendant at the Maintop masthead
    That for the Second a White
    That for the Third a Blue
    That for the Fourth a Yellow
Which the following are to hoist as soon as they are at anchor, but not

FIRST DIVISION
Exeter Sloop Fly Sloop and Royal George. Transports – Cutters

Ships	Masters	Guns	Seamen	Regiments on Board
Gloucester	John Gorman	12	26	
Friendship	John Sedgwell	10	24	Royals (1st)
Susanna and Sarah	William Leslie	16	29	
Loyalty	John Gibson	9	20	
Peter and Mary	Thomas Aslington	18	32	
Creighton	Jason Loyd	14	29	Frampton's (30th)
New Industry	Geoffrey Wigg	20	26	
Winchester	Elias Legrass	20	46	

SECOND DIVISION
Devonshire, Tilbury, Tavistock. Sloops – Transports

Ships	Masters	Guns	Seamen	Regiments on Board
Duke of Cumberland	Joseph Major	22	23	
Buckhanan	Hugh Craford	18	32	Harrison's (15th)
Sandwich	Thomas Haselwood	20	29	
Industry	Charles Gainford	9	20	
Liberty	William Hill	9	31	
Hope	Nathaniel Pickering	9	28	High-
Triton	Jacob Hailles	8	18	landers
York	Thomas Story	16	26	(42nd)

before, and to keep them abroad till the several senior Captains in the Division they belong to have anchored.

They are to be berthed near the place where the senior Captains of each Division drop their anchor always: always spreading such distance from each other as the road and harbour will permit.

In the absence of the senior Captain the next Captain of the Division is required to take this particular care and charge upon him, and accordingly in the same manner to hoist and wear the same marks of Distinction.

THIRD DIVISION
Hastings, York, Mortar-Bomb, Post Boy. Tender – Transports

Ships	Masters	Guns	Seamen	Regiments on Board
Dorsetshire	Richard Brown	28	28	
Vernon	Francis Mitchelson	16	24	Bragg's
Adventurer	Thomas Bagly	8	24	(28th)
Royal William	Robert Bowman	8	16	
Richmond	James Frazor	20	24	
Liberty	William Long	9	31	
Prince Fredrick	Geoffrey Payne	12	20	Richbell's
Content	William Storry	8	24	(39th)
Adventure 2nd	John Barnard	8	16	

FOURTH DIVISION
Sapphire, Scipio & Vulcan. fire ships. Tavistock. Brigs and Tenders

Ordinance Store Ships			
Westmorland	Jason Shanks		Marines
Bosphorus	Jason Kenard		Colonel Holmes
Boston	Geoffrey Calcutt	Companies of	Party
Landovery	John Stone	Artillery on	
Susanna and Sarah	Okey Belford	Board the Seven Store Ships	Colonel Jeffreys' Party
Esther	John Herron		Colonel Byng's
Neptune	John Gouger		Party

The Admiral – Ruby – Tilbury – Edinburgh together with the Marlborough, Baltimore, Mary Gally, Nathaniel and John, transports are to anchor in the middle for the convenient passage of the boats.

When the senior Captain would speak with any of the masters of the several transports or store ships in his Division, he will spread an ensign in the mizen shrouds and fire a gun, but when I make that signal all the masters of all transports, and store ships, are to come on board me. . . .

> Dated on Board the *Princessa* Man of War
> September 16th. 1746

> By Command of the Admiral. . . . .

SATURDAY 20th
The *Sapphire* and *Man of War* sloop run inshore and fired upon them: they retreated in great numbers.

SUNDAY 21st
Early in the morning they fired on our fleet again; the *Sapphire* and sloop fired very smartly, and drove them from their battery. The Admiral ordered the long boats to be manned and armed with sailors. They went ashore and took possession of the two guns on the battery, then proceeded in a body to a house where a number of Capuchins were assembled, surprised them, went to some villages and took two small sloops. General St Clair marched up the country with the foot, the artillery disembarked with three brass three pounders and six Coehorn mortars with stores and drew them up a hill about one mile from the riverside with about six hundred marines.

MONDAY 22nd
Pitched a laboratory tent, mounted a guard of artillery and brought up the two brass guns belonging to the French. At 3 pm Captain Chalmers and Lieutenant Northall with a detachment marched with three brass three pounders, with marines to draw the guns in men's harness. Came to a village called Ploermel about 4 miles from Fort L'Orient; the peasants fled from this place yesterday after a stout resistance. We lost a few men in the engagement. General St Clair had possession; the artillery lay in a large church called St Peter's.

TUESDAY 23rd
Captain Chalmers, Lieutenant Northall with the party of artillery, marched at 6 am, joined General St Clair and the army on a hill about two miles from Fort L'Orient and three miles from Port Louis. A

strong garrison of about 500 marines were left with the other part of artillery to take care of the stores. The Town Major and his attendants with a trumpeter came to offer terms of capitulation, which was if General St Clair would withdraw his army they would raise a contribution of one hundred thousand pounds sterling, which was rejected by the General. He gave the Major for answer he intended to distribute a much larger sum amongst his soldiers in case he had the possession of the fort, which he told them he did not despair of, and that two million sterling would be the least sum he should comply with. The Major replied he would give an answer the next morning, but the General replied he would give no longer time than three hours to consult and sent a drummer of General Bragg's with the French Major and in less than three hours the Governor of Fort L'Orient and the drummer of Bragg's came back. When the General perceived that such a sum would not be complied with and that they would defend themselves in the best manner they could, the rest of the artillery came up to us with Captain Farquharson. Pitched a Laboratory tent, and planted our guns over the river on a high hill. Landed one ten-inch brass mortar, two iron twelve-pounders and mounted them on carriages. Lieutenant Macleod of the artillery with a detachment was ordered to follow and join the army. Commodore Coats had ordered about 500 sailors from the men of war to draw in harness and assist all they could. At 9 am General St Clair with his ADCs came to the ground where the remainder of the stores was and ordered Captain Farquharson with a detachment of artillery and ammunition to march immediately to the army. Lieutenant Macleod and his party joined us.

WEDNESDAY 24th

About 12 noon about two miles from Fort L'Orient, General St Clair had pitched his quarters. The Foot were employed in making roads and breaking down walls for the foot to march abreast. About 4 pm a party of our army engaged with the peasants in a small wood and fired small shot very briskly, which made the French retreat; an officer of Bragg's was wounded with a musket ball in the thigh. Came to our ground again. All still and quiet. The Foot employed in making fascines etc. Our engineers fixing on the ground to erect a battery. The French firing from a small battery – some few cannon shot. About 6 pm this evening the Foot began to carry down the fascines etc. and they were set to work immediately entrenching and making the battery by the directions of our Engineers.

Thursday 25th

About 3 am a party of artillery marched to the battery with one ten-inch brass mortar and two iron 12-pounders. About 5 am the battery completed dismounting the mortar, fixed her and planted our guns about $1\frac{1}{2}$ miles from Fort L'Orient and made a magazine for powder and stores. About 7 am loaded the mortar with a carcass which fell near a large church in the centre of the town. Immediately the French began from three batteries; right and left and a battery in the centre. We kept firing our mortar once every 30 minutes till near noon, the French firing very warmly from their batteries and from a small sloop in the river. They fired barred shot and cannon shot from 18, 12, 6 and 3 pounders. We set several houses on fire with our carcasses but they soon extinguished them, as supposed by a machine or engine. Soon after 12 noon we saw from our battery a large number of the peasants marching down a large street and about 200 of them on the other side of the town to the left of us; those on the left headed by a man in his shirt waving his hat to those on the right to advance to our battery (This sham captain was supposed to be a deserter from Bragg's regiment the night before.)

They came on very briskly towards the battery with great assurance. Captain Farquharson ordered the Foot to get their arms, but when called upon, the party who had been employed in the night at our battery had left their arms with the other part of the regiment. The small party of the artillery was lodged in a house about 200 yards from the battery, and the French, advancing so briskly on us, put us to some little confusion. Captain Farquharson immediately advanced towards them with one Corporal and one mattross and ten of the Highlanders joined them. Some men of the Royal Scots made their retreat after exchanging several volleys. In their retreat a musket ball killed the supposed deserter of Bragg's. We followed them within 200 yards of the skirts of the fort. The French began firing from their batteries again as fast as they could load and fire and had brought their guns to bear on our battery, but did no execution. A large number assembled together soon after their retreat. Captain Farquharson ordered one of our 12-pounders to be loaded with grape, fired on them and supposedly did great execution, for they immediately retreated into a large building, in a direct line with our battery and considerably nearer than their former battery; they pulled down the place where they had been erecting a breastwork and mounted two guns. We fired amongst them, and they dispersed to some other houses. We continued firing shells and carcasses about two in an hour, best part of the day and four rounds of shot an hour. Major Bagshaw of Richbell's Regiment received a cannon shot in his thigh. Surgeon Butler of the Artillery immediately cut off his leg and thigh, tied up the arteries and took horse to send a party of Grenadiers to take the Major off. They crept by a small wallside, and then on their hands and knees, and carried him to the village where General St Clair's HQ was, who sent him on board the hospital ship. He is in a fair way of recovery.

About 7 pm a party of French advanced near our battery, and fired upon some of Frampton's Regiment which being returned by our parties and Frampton's, the French directly fired a round of cannon from four different batteries, some 24, 18, 12 and 6 pounders. A party of Royal Scots immediately after the volleys of small arms, was drawn up in the centre of our battery six deep, and several parties of different regiments drawn up in order to work at the repairs of our battery, being sunk in some places two foot or more, and very much shattered with the French firing all day. Our engineers settled the Foot to work on enlarging the trenches. All very still on both sides all that night.

FRIDAY 26th

About 4 am we had two 12-pounders brought to the battery by the sailors and fixed them to the embrasures, so that we had four 12-pounders and one ten-inch mortar. The French began to fire at us about 5 am. Our first fire was a carcass and the French immediately fired a round of shot from five batteries, they having erected a fresh battery on Thursday night and Friday morning, and they had planted a mortar on the new battery. Continued firing on each side, the French as fast as they could load, we firing with a great deal of reluctance for fear of wanting ammunition before it could be brought from our first ground. About 9 am we fired a round of red hot shot, fired carcasses and shells 4 in an hour. About 12 a 7-inch shell fell on the face of our bastion and demolished that part of our battery, wounded a sailor and several of the artillery, blew up the chair that Captain Farquharson sat on. Did no other damage. About 1 pm Captain Farquharson sent to know if any more stores was come, and about two the messenger returned with ammunition cart and sundry stores, shells etc, with orders from General St Clair to Captain Farquharson to fire our mortar and guns as fast as we could load. The French fired at least three shot for our one, they having at least 12 pieces of cannon and we but 4 and so much nearer to us than we to the town, where we were designed to do execution. About 2 pm Thomas Collins, mattross, was shot by a 12-pounder. It took him in the side and came out at the back of his head. Continued firing on both sides very smartly, demolished several houses of the town of Fort L'Orient. About 5 pm a party of the French disguised in Highlanders' dress, about 50 in number, advancing towards our battery, fired several small shot at our men that was entrenched. We at the battery thought they were our own Highlanders, but when we understood that they were French in disguise, we fired two of our guns loaded with grapeshot amongst them and made them retreat. They killed but two of our foot. At that time the French were firing with carcasses, shells and some rounds of cannon shot until near 7 pm. The French left off about 6.30 pm. About 9 pm General St Clair ordered three brass three pounders and a party of artillery to be detached. We expected they had agreed to attack Fort L'Orient by storm. At the same time the foot had orders to strike their tents, and to draw up. Soon after a three-pounder gun was drawn and marched at the head of a regiment of foot and two in the rear, and the 3 three-pounders at the head of two other regiments. Orders were sent by the General about 7 to spike up our four 12-pounders and to bring off our mortar, but the sailors from the men of war, who were designed for this part of duty, had left us and straggled to different places, and the foot who was to guard the artillery in the retreat being not sufficient to draw such a large piece of ordnance, was obliged to spike up our mortar and leave it with such stores as spades and shovels etc. Retreated without the least confusion from the battery and came up to the General's Quarters where we had about 4 barrels of gunpowder. Engineer Armstrong, our Commander of the Artillery, ordered it to be blown up by setting the houses on fire some little distance from the powder. The first part of the army in their retreat halted at Ploermel until the rear came up, then the whole marched. Came to our former ground where we had left some artillery stores etc with a guard of marines who were much fatigued with hard duty.

SATURDAY 27th
At 2 am we had orders to ground and to lie on our arms until daylight, very heavy rains and blustery weather; about noon ordered to get the remainder of our guns and stores to the riverside: put some on board that night. Embarked two regiments of foot and some artillery people: the remainder of the forces pitched tents on a rock, and when the tide came in they were surrounded by the sea.

SUNDAY 28th
The outpost sentries thought they had seen some of the French in a great body watching us in the night which caused us all to be on our guard but when it was light saw nothing of them. Harrison's embarked

about 4 am, the artillery about 5 in men of wars boats. Some marines
putting off in order to reach their respective men of war in a long boat
overset with about 50 of them which occasioned the loss of about 29.
The others were taken up by the assistance of several other boats; the
whole embarked by 12 noon.

MONDAY 29th
Captain Chalmers and part of his company came on board. At 6 pm
hove our anchor and ran further out.

TUESDAY 30th
A signal for sailing and was all ready for sailing by 6 pm.

WEDNESDAY OCTOBER 1st WNW

Several ships joined us at noon and a French ship of 64 guns, taken
by HMS *Exeter* and *Poole*. At 4 pm all the fleet plying to the windward
of Quiberon Bay. At 8 anchored near the Admiral. The gales ended
and fine weather prevailed.

FRIDAY 3rd
Sailed nearer the Bay of Quiberon.

SATURDAY 4th
The *Exeter* and *Poole* men of war drove on shore amongst the rocks,
the French fired several shots from a battery on a rock of two iron
24-pounders. About 10 am the Highlanders disembarked and some
foot and marines lay in several churches and villages, the French
running away to a strong town at the other side of the river, about 3
leagues from where we embarked. A very poor part of the country –
nothing to be seen, only old rags.

SUNDAY 5th
Disembarked all our artillery, Highlanders and Royals. Pitched tents
and mounted a piquet guard on a very high hill about two miles from
the town where the French ran for shelter.

MONDAY 6th
The artillery lay in a village near the riverside. Part of the artillery
marched to the hill, another part of the artillery went round the
country and found 18 guns of iron ordnance: some 24, 18, 9 and 6
pounders. Began to form a battery between two rivers, about half a

mile space of land at low water. About 10 am relieved by a party of
marines. obliged to make the battery of seaweeds, and hogsheads. No
brushwood about this part: mounted a guard of artillery. Pitched all
the tents on a high hill in view of the French, our army lying in
villages near at hand, the weather very cold and no wood to make
fires.

TUESDAY 7th
Finished making the battery and entrenchments, brought 4 guns and
mounted them at the battery. About 3 pm the French commissary
came with several long boats to exchange prisoners from Fort L'Orient
which lay about 10 leagues from Quiberon. We made redoubts half a
mile forward from our battery for our advance guard.

WEDNESDAY 8th
Brought 3 more guns from the furthest part of the island[3] to the battery
and mounted them. Got a great quantity of ammunition and 18 or 20
brass pieces of ordnance and sent them on board the men of war. Only
the powder we kept for use. About 12 noon 18 or 20 of the French
on horseback advanced near our outguard; supposed to be Engineers
etc, retreated soon again. Engineer Armstrong, Captain Chalmers,
Lieutenant Picke and 24 of the artillery, went round the island,
dismounted all their guns in the batteries and broke their trunnions.
The sailors set on fire the French man of war that was plundered of
its guns, and other things, which was contrary to the General's orders.
Several confined for the same.

THURSDAY 9th
The French sent terms of capitulation which was received by the
General's ADC. But the General refusing it, ordered a party of
artillery to go round the island, and break the trunnions of all the
ordnance they could find, and to set all their carriages on fire which
was immediately put in execution.

FRIDAY 10th
In the evening the foot struck their tents, except the piquet guard and
some few of the artillery. Some of the foot embarked and some artillery
people. About 8 pm our sailors set on fire several of their villages and
burnt several of their fishing boats and other boats that could not be
got out of their harbour.

[3] The Quiberon peninsula which Wood thought was an island.

SATURDAY 11th

Dismounted the guns at our battery, broke the trunnions and blew up one 24-pounder iron gun and buried a great quantity of their shot etc. The whole embarked by 1. At noon the men of war fired their guns, it being the King's Coronation. This island very barren: no fruit, little cattle, scarce of fresh water and provisions, the people chiefly supported by their fishing, the French very few, met with no repulse at all.

SUNDAY 12th ESE

At 8 am a signal for sailing. At 10 we sailed with pleasant weather at 1 pm cast anchor in 12 fathom distance 4 miles from the Isle of Houat and about 6 miles from the Isle of Hoedic.

MONDAY 13th

At 9 am the men-of-war sailors went to take the island, and two men of war went to engage the castle and after firing a few shots they surrendered the castle of Houat, and at 2 pm they surrendered the castle of Hoedic.

TUESDAY 14th

At 6 am a signal on board the Admiral for the engineers, they receiving orders to go immediately and blow up all the fortifications and the two castles: a party of the artillery immediately disembarked and met with a few invalids; very poor, who got their living chiefly by fishing. About 10 am began to undermine the castle of Houat and the works around it; another party ordered to Hoedic and likewise to undermine the castle and works around it: a party of sailors ordered to a fortification, and to blow it up as soon as possible, it being but small they got it ready for blowing by the next day but some of the sailors stood too near when it was blown up, that some of the stones wounded several of them and took a leg off from a Lieutenant of one of the men of war. The other parties worked hard all day and all night.

WEDNESDAY 15th

Blew up the castle of Hoedic and the other party hard at work at Houat castle blew up the outworks of Houat castle with 4 barrels of gun powder and in the evening blew up the castle with 8 barrels. About 8 set the ruins of the castle on fire, and carriages of guns, the long boats coming for us, we all got safe to our respective ships by 9 pm.

FRIDAY 17th ENE

A signal for sailing and at 11 am we were all under sail; laid to for some of the ships that could not weather the island of Belleisle until about 4 pm. 41 sail in company.

SATURDAY, SUNDAY & MONDAY

Pleasant weather, but about 2 am Monday morning we had violent squalls of wind and rain which continued for six or seven days, the wind being likewise foul until 27th in the morning, when the wind coming SBW which was fair for us.

TUESDAY 28th

Came in sight of the Irish shore at 1.30 pm.

WEDNESDAY 29th

Cast anchor at a placed called the cove of Cork at 2 pm.

FRIDAY 31st

Weighed anchor and sailed to a place called Passage about 7 miles from Cork.

WEDNESDAY NOVEMBER 12th

Disembarked our troops, and artillery and came to quarters at Cork; left a command of 14 men of the artillery to take care of the store ships which was to be relieved every fortnight.

IN THE COCKPIT OF EUROPE

1747–8

NARRATIVE

B ETWEEN 12 January and 25 April, 1747, John Chalmers' company moved by sea from their barracks in Cork to join the four other Royal Artillery companies encamped under the allied Commander-in-Chief, William, Duke of Cumberland, alongside the Dutch, Austrian, Hanoverian and Hessian contingents in Holland between Breda and Antwerp. The Royal Artillery was under command of Colonel William Belford, whose handling of the light field guns at Culloden had contributed so mightily to the outcome of that battle.

The sea journey was painfully slow. General Fuller's brigade of infantry which also came from service at L'Orient disembarked at Flushing to find many of their tents rendered unserviceable by the rats in the ships' holds and their camp kettles rusted through from the action of the sea water. Despite the state of its equipment the brigade was ordered straight into action by Cumberland, to help defend the south bank of the Scheldt under command of an elderly Dutch General, De La Rocque. The Royals, Lord John Murray's Highlanders and Bragg's [48th] were in a sharp action near Hulst, the Royals in particular losing many men. Chalmers' company heard the bad news about their colleagues almost immediately after landing.

French control of the navigation of the Scheldt gravely affected Cumberland's line of communications, and the difficulty of moving supplies forward constrained his ability to act against Marshall Saxe. Saxe slowly built up a force considerably superior to the allies in the area of Louvain, with his left holding Antwerp and threatening Bergen-op-Zoom and his right deployed south-west of the important fortress of Maastricht on the Meuse.

Not only was Cumberland disheartened at the failure of his Dutch and Austrian allies to produce the numbers for his army that the negotiations during the winter of 1746/7 had led him to expect, but he also complained at the lack of strategic direction from London. In consequence he hesitated between counterattacking on the Scheldt to free his communications across the channel and committing himself to the defence of the Meuse valley down which came the Austrian supplies and reinforcements through the territory of Liège and Luxembourg.

Meanwhile, behind the River Dyle Saxe lay in his cantonments in the belief that Cumberland's supply difficulties would so weaken the allies by the autumn that he would have won the campaign without risking an attack. Chalmers' company with the rest of the Royal Artillery almost always camped alongside Cumberland's headquarters so that Wood had considerable knowledge of the army's plans. The company was responsible for manning six 9-pounder brass guns in the artillery train, which by 1747 was considerably more powerful than in 1745 at Fontenoy. In addition to Chalmers' guns, there were six 12-pounders, fourteen 6-pounders, two 8" howitzers and six 10" mortars. Royal Artillery personnel from the companies also supervised and partly manned the fourteen 3-pounders and twelve short 6-pounders which were deployed in pairs to each infantry battalion in battle.

From Wood's narrative it appears that men from Chalmers' company were detached to the infantry. Though the guns of the company were generally grouped in batteries, the company establishment was probably divided into a Headquarters and three sections each of two 9-pounders, there being one Captain/Lieutenant, three subaltern officers, three Lieutenant Fireworkers, three sergeants, three corporals and nine bombardiers. The rank and file consisted of twenty-four gunners, making four to a gun, and sixty-eight mattrosses.

Chalmers probably kept Wood as a volunteer at his headquarters along with the two drummers, clerks of stores, engineers and artificers. When ordered to send men to the infantry with the lighter guns the company was responsible for finding one subaltern officer, two NCOs and eight mattrosses for every two battalions. Each battalion produced nine of its own men for its allotted two-gun section which took post in the front line on a flank.

Until King Louis XV arrived at Marshall Saxe's headquarters in the field early in June there was little more than skirmishing between opposing outposts. Wood's diary gives a vivid impression of the routine of the camp and Cumberland's efforts at training his polyglot army. From London, George II exhibited some nervousness that his son might attempt some rash attack across the Dyle and urged restraint.

Suddenly, towards the middle of June, Saxe concentrated an isolated corps within striking distance of Maastricht. Cumberland at once reacted to the bait but failed to move his ill-coordinated allied columns in sufficient time to produce a superior force against the French advanced corps. By a remarkable forced march Saxe established a numerical superiority at the point of contact and on Sunday, 21 June broke through the left centre of Cumberland's line before Maastricht.

The Royal Artillery had been carefully deployed in positions defiladed from the front behind wooded villages and wreaked enormous havoc against the dense columns of the French attack as the packed regiments surged forward and back in a succession of closely pressed assaults on the allied left. At the height of the battle Cumberland ordered his whole line to advance but the Austrians on his right were either unable or unwilling to join in and a Dutch cavalry regiment, unable to stand the fire, broke back through the hinge of the allied line making a gap which the French did not fail to exploit.

In the subsequent retreat on Maastricht, the Royal Artillery had to abandon several of their guns and a number of prisoners. From Wood's account it was their heaviest action ever. His simple factual report gives a new insight into one of the greatest mass encounters between 18th century armies. Saxe mustered some 80–90,000 men against the 70–80,000 men of the allies. Though neither side was fully engaged, yet the huge losses Saxe sustained through his bludgeoning attacks caused the disillusioned Louis XV to urge peace upon England who, as he said "not only fought all, but paid all". Saxe failed in his immediate object and the allies withdrew safely under the guns of Maastricht across the Meuse where they encamped for many weeks opposite the French along the river bank.

Saxe now strengthened his left. His subordinate corps commander, the Danish mercenary Lowendal, opened a formal attack on the fortress of Bergen-op-Zoom. Cumberland sent away gunners, engineers, and infantry to assist the garrison, but Lieutenant Abraham Tovey R A and his detachment from Chalmers' company arrived too late. Other gunners went direct from Woolwich. The fall of Bergen after two months' siege shocked all Europe. The taking of such a place made a much greater impact than the battle outside Maastricht. The only successes for England that year were gained at sea and Wood describes the *feu de joie* fired in honour of Admiral Anson's famous victory off Finisterre in the month of May.

Throughout the winter and following spring Wood describes in some detail the humdrum activities of life in the cantonments and the move out to the defence of Maastricht.

Following upon the earlier moves for peace after the Battle of Laufeld preliminary negotiations were begun at Liège and then Aix-la-Chapelle in 1748. To Cumberland's indignation the French plenipotentiaries prevaricated until Saxe was able to enter Maastricht with his greatly superior force. Diplomatic discussions between the parties went on at Aix long after the Preliminaries of Peace were initialled on 30 April. It was not until November that Cumberland was able to bring home his troops and for much of the intervening time he was fearful that Saxe would march against him to exact more favourable terms. Considering how badly the war had gone in the Low Countries for England, Austria and Holland from 1744 to 1748, it was remarkable that the peace terms agreed were on the "status quo ante" as far as England was concerned. To achieve this, France had expended enormous resources on land and lost heavily in commercial and naval strength at sea. If the long period of hanging about in 1748 by the five companies of the Royal Artillery enabled Wood to record for us much of the day-to-day life of the regiment in the field, it also allowed Cumberland's military artist David Morier[1] to produce for his collection an unique documentary painting of the much strengthened and improved English field artillery train.

It is notable that Wood throughout the period utters hardly a single grumble or complaint, tells us nothing of his personal life and makes no criticism of colleagues or superiors. He records only that food was lacking on the eve of the only big battle he ever engaged in, at Laufeldt, but for our knowledge of the professional English gunner in the mid-eighteenth century his contribution is unique.

In consequence of his campaign experiences from 1743 to 1748 Cumberland took an increasing interest in the Royal Regiment. He called for experiments to improve the weapons by setting up a private foundry in Chelsea employing a Saxon gunmaker; he ordered competitive firing tests in Windsor Park which convinced him that the British guns were the most effective. With his father, he inaugurated annual inspections of the Royal Regiment in Hyde Park. He also persuaded the King to agree to grant commissions, without the opportunity to purchase, to gunner officers and to give them army rank from 1751. Thus artillery officers began to play a more general part in the activity of the army as a whole, rather than remaining a Board of Ordnance preserve. Desaguliers, a highly scientific gunner officer of Huguenot origin, was made responsible for the magnificent firework display in the Green Park which was held to celebrate the peace of 1748. Handel, an even more famous immigrant, composed the accompanying music. Maybe Wood and his friends from Woolwich went up to London to see the fun.

[1] David Morier 1705–1770. A Swiss artist brought to England by the Duke of Cumberland who paid him £200 a year.

The Netherlands

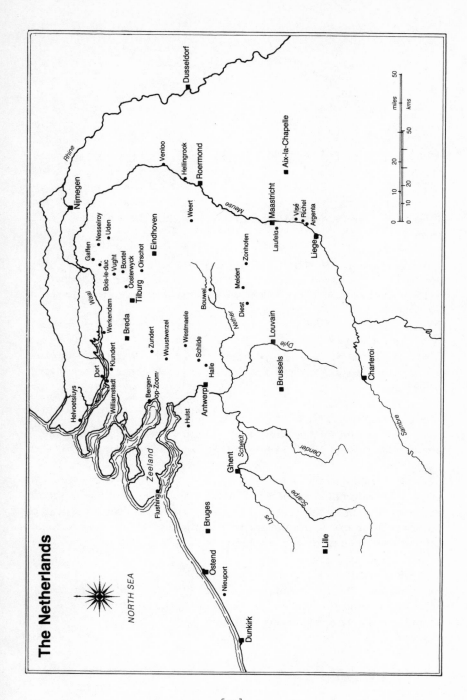

NORTH SEA

Dunkirk
Nieuport
Ostend
Bruges
Flushing
Zeeland
Helvoetsluys
Williamstadt
Dort
Waal
Rhine
Nijmegen
Gaffen
Nesselroy
Uden
Bois-le-duc
Vught
Boxtel
Oosterwyck
Olirschot
Tilburg
Breda
Klundert
Werkendam
Bergen-op-Zoom
Zundert
Wuustwerzel
Hulst
Antwerp
Schilde
Westmaele
Halle
Ghent
Lille
Dender
Scheldt
Scarpe
Lys
Bruwel
Nether
Diest
Meldert
Zonhofen
Louvain
Dyle
Brussels
Charleroi
Sambre
Eindhoven
Weert
Venloo
Hellingrook
Roermond
Meuse
Maastricht
Visé
Richel
Argenta
Laufeld
Liege
Aix-la-Chapelle
Dusseldorf

miles
kms
0   10   20   50
0   20   50

[31]

IN THE COCKPIT OF EUROPE 1747/8

JANUARY 12th 1747
Orders came to General St Clair to embark when the *Ruby* man of war came in.

JANUARY 15th, 16th, 17th, AND 18th
Embarking all our forces and all got safe on board their respective ships. In the company of artillery we lessened Ireland of the burden of 28 ladies.

JANUARY 23rd
The wind being NBW unmoored and sailed to the cove of Cork; came to anchor near the *Ruby* and *Sapphire* men of war about half an hour after 7 am.

FEBRUARY 10th
A signal for unmooring; unmoored and got all ready for sailing but the wind turned southerly; obliged them all to moor again.

FEBRUARY 12th NBE
A signal for unmooring the wind being NNW. Unmoored and got all ready for sailing by the next morning, but the wind turned SE; obliged us all to moor again, and the weather being very windy obliged them all to strike their yards and top masts.

FEBRUARY 16th NBE
A signal for unmooring, the wind being NBE was ready by 12, the signal for sailing for our convoy, as likewise the convoy of the West India fleet the wind being fair for them.

FEBRUARY 17th NBE
Came in sight of the islands of Scilly which are about 7 leagues from
the Land's End of England: kept from land all that night.

FEBRUARY 19th E
Came in sight of land about 6 am about 10 leagues from Crookhaven,
and at 12 noon hung out our ensign for a pilot. As soon as he was on
board steered for Crookhaven harbour. About 3 pm cast anchor in 5
fathom; at 4 pm one of the transports called the *Friend* ran against the
Westmoreland, tore a hole in the side of our ship, broke the fluke of
their small bower anchor and received great damage.

CROOKHAVEN HARBOUR
A very poor miserable part of the country; they get their living chiefly
by fishing for pilchards and barrelling them up; they live in nothing
but huts made of straw and clay; the country very rocky.

MARCH 8th NW
The wind being fair a signal for sailing, but about 4 pm the wind
turned easterly which obliged them all to moor again.

MARCH 10th NNW
A signal for weighing anchor, and sailed about 4 pm, it being very
pleasant weather all that night.

MARCH 12th
About 10 am came in sight of the rocks of Scilly, the wind continuing
about west.

MARCH 15th
Came in sight of Land's End of England but about 8 am the wind
turned SE which obliged all the fleet to bear back for Scilly; at 11 am
hung out a signal for a pilot; about 12 he came on board. Came to
anchor about 2 pm in the harbour.

SCILLY HARBOUR
A very dangerous harbour going in, but when once in you are
surrounded with rocks; a tolerably good fortification when the new
works will be finished that they are about. It faces the passage coming
in.

March 21st NNW

About 8 am a signal to prepare for sailing and at 10 am the pilot came on board and sailed safe out of the harbour; at 12 noon came in sight of the Land's End of England.

March 22nd

About 4 am the wind turned ENE (which was quite foul), which obliged the fleet to beat about, still keeping in sight of England, but about 9 am the wind turned NW and bore for England. About 12 noon came in sight of the mainland and at 6 pm passed Mount's Bay.

March 23rd

Came into the English Channel and at 10 am came in sight of the Eddystone and about 12 noon came in sight of Plymouth Sound.

March 24th

Parted with Frampton's Regiment at Plymouth: the rest of the fleet bore away for Spithead.

March 25th

Came in sight of the Isle of Wight about 12 noon and at 4 pm ten sail of shipping parted from us to go for the Downs with the *Ruby* man of war to convoy them. We came to an anchor at St Helens at 11 pm.

March 28th

Orders for Richbell's [Regiment] to disembark and about 4 the whole regiment was disembarked and landed at Portsmouth.

March 29th

The company of artillery was all ordered to leave the seven store ships, and to embark on board the *Richmond*, which was prepared for us to sail for Flanders.

March 30th

30 sail of ships came into St Helens from the Downs where they came to an anchor.

April 5th

The wind coming WBS a signal for sailing and got under sail by 6 pm and sailed with pleasant weather all that night towards the Downs. Convoy was HMS *Sapphire*.

APRIL 7th
Came in sight of Beachy Head about 6 am.

APRIL 11th
Came in sight of the South Foreland and about 10 am cast anchor in Dover Road as did all the rest of the fleet.

APRIL 12th
About 12 noon the pilot came on board to pilot us to Holland and at 1 pm a signal for weighing on board; our convoy the *Sapphire*. Sailed about 3 pm but the wind turned E; came to an anchor. About 6 pm the wind turned SE: signal for sailing and at 8 pm sailed with pleasant weather all that night.

APRIL 13th
About 10 am came in sight of Dunkirk and Nieuport. About 4 pm, the tide turning, the Commodore fired a gun for anchoring and came to an anchor about 7 leagues from Ostend. At 10 pm a signal for sailing; were under sail by 11 pm.

APRIL 14th
About 8 am came in sight of Flushing road, where was Commodore Mitchell with seven sail of men of war who saluted our Commodore which was returned. There was a large army of French seen the other side: both foot and horse, with several fishing boats to land their forces, if an opportunity should serve to make a descent on Flushing town.

APRIL 15th
One of our ships took seven of the French fishing boats and carried them into the harbour of Flushing. About 1 pm fired the battery guns: it being the Duke of Cumberland's birthday. Great rejoicing in the town of Flushing by the Dutch upon the said occasion.

APRIL 17th
About 9 pm the *Sapphire*'s boat came along side all the shipping with orders to be on our guard for they had espied several boats which they expected to be loaded with French soldiers for to land in the Isle of Zeeland. Accordingly we loaded the ships' guns and placed double watches as did all the rest of the fleet, but in the morning saw nothing of them.

April 18th

An express came from the Duke of Cumberland to land the three regiments in Flushing town viz: the Royals, Highlanders and Braggs', and the artillery to sail for Williamstadt. Immediately a signal for sailing on board our convoy, the *Kingfisher* sloop. Sailed about 7 pm and came to an anchor at 8.30 pm about a league from the town of Flushing.

April 20th

Sailed by 4 am came to an anchor at 10, the wind at EBN. At 5 a signal for sailing and in weighing we lost our best bower anchor (on starboard side) and 14 fathom of her cable. Fired a gun to bring our convoy to and to let them know we had lost our anchor. We sailed all that night, wind at EBN, quite foul.

April 21st

About 7 am our ship struck twice on the sands, but happily did no damage; sailed all that day. Scarcely any wind and made but little way.

April 22nd

Came in sight of Helvoetsluys about 3 pm and at 6 pm our convoy made a signal to part with us. We fired 9 guns to salute him, he returned the compliment with 7. We came to an anchor at 9 pm in Helvoetsluys harbour.

April 23rd

A Dutch pilot came on board and about 8 am we weighed anchor and lay to for Captain Chalmers, Captain Farquharson and the Captain of the ship. At 10 am they came on board. We made sail directly, the wind being SE and pleasant weather with land on each side of us. Passed by several pleasant towns by the riverside, the tide being done came to an anchor within 3 leagues of Williamstadt. At low tide the water is quite fresh. About 8 pm the wind blew fresh against us, which obliged us to keep to an anchor all night and wait for the next tide. Captain Chalmers, Captain Farquharson, Engineer Clarke[2] with four of our artillery men rowed to Williamstadt about 10 pm. Mr Buck, mattross, was missing in the third watch. Looked all over the ship. Could not find him. We supposed that as he went to the heads of the

---

[2] Clarke was the engineer who accompanied the ill-fated expedition against La Rochelle in 1757.

ship to ease himself he fell overboard. He was about 45 years of age, and had about £50 a year besides his pay.

APRIL 24th
Weighed anchor about 9 am and sailed with the tide, but about 10 am came to anchor 1 mile from Williamstadt, and sent all the officers' baggage on shore, and sent an express to the Duke of Cumberland.

APRIL 25th
Disembarked all the artillery and stores and waited the return of the express from the Duke.

APRIL 27th
Some of the Royal Scots came here: they had had an engagement with the French, the 25th, on the island of Zeeland – where they had a great many of their regiment killed and wounded – there was not about two hundred left.[3]

APRIL 28th
About 11 am the express arrived from the Duke, with orders to march directly and about 11 am left Williamstadt. Came to Klundert at 6 pm. $4\frac{1}{2}$ miles; ferried over the water and at 8 pm came to Sevenbergen which is $4\frac{1}{2}$ miles from Klundert. Lay there that night.

APRIL 29th
Came to Deleur by 9 am – 5 miles. Crossed the ferry and marched to Fater by 12 noon which is 6 miles. Marched on and came to Zundert by 1 pm which is 3 miles where we had quarters and remained there all night.

APRIL 30th
Marched by 8 am and came to halt at Wuustwerzel, which is 6 miles from Zundert. General Woolfenbuttel had quarters there. He is General of one of the regiments belonging to the Emperor. Marched by 2 pm and came to camp by 6 pm which is about 7 miles from Wuustwerzel. Pitched our tents along with our own artillery which consisted of five companies. The English at the left of the Camp and the Emperor's on the right. We had about 64 pieces of brass cannon. This camp was called Westmaele, it being the name of the Duke's

---

[3] This engagement was at Fort Sandberg outside Hulst.

quarters. The names of the camps generally go by the name of the Headquarters.

MAY 2nd
Orders from the Duke to have 12 pieces of 3-pounders in readiness. Marched about 1 pm from here to go to a place called the Halle.

MAY 3rd
The five companies went to hear prayers and sermon, which was performed in a laboratory tent. At 2 pm orders came for to strike our tents, as did all the other troops. Marched by 3 pm, halted at 8 pm and pitched our tents, marched about 7 miles: Schilde camp, the Duke's quarters.

MAY 4th SCHILDE CAMP
Orders came for to fire three rounds of 21 guns on account of some rejoicing with a running fire from the infantry taking the fire from the right of the camp which was performed after sunset.[4]

MAY 6th
Orders to strike our tents and marched by 7 am two miles nearer the right of the army, and pitched our tents on a heath by 9 am.

MAY 8th
Two short 6-pounders with a detachment of artillery had orders to go and relieve the other command of artillery with two guns, which was about 4 miles from here.

MAY 12th
The Muster Roll was called by 4 am. It was called throughout the camp on account of a house that was broken into and robbed and two men that lived in the house were killed but it was not found out, as I hear.

MAY 14th
Orders to march by 4 am. Marched until 6 pm, Bouwel Camp.

MAY 18th
A command marched from Bouwel camp with two short six pounders. 16 mattrosses, 1 Sergeant, 1 Corporal and 2 gunners.

[4] To salute the birth of an Austrian Prince.

MAY 19th BOUWEL CAMP
Marched from here another command of three six pounders, mattrosses, gunners and bombardiers.

MAY 20th
A command of 70 men belonging to the artillery went on a foraging party; came back by 6 pm. The three 6-pounders returned by 8 pm.

MAY 22nd
A review of part of our artillery, with 8 pieces of our short 6-pounders and four regiments of foot which were Conway's [48th], Douglas's [32nd], Crawford's [25th] and Dejean's [37th] regiments. The Duke came about 10 am to review us. Fired about 60 rounds from our guns and was done about 1 pm.

MAY 23rd
A command of 4 short 6-pounders marched from here by 6 am to relieve the other party of artillery that had two pieces of cannon at a town called Lier. They came here by 2 pm.

MAY 24th
News came to the Duke that Admiral Anson had taken six men of war from the French.[5] On that account our train was ordered to fire which was performed after sunset, the Austrians fired 30 pieces of cannon at the right of the camp, the Hanoverians 30 and the English 21, and a running fire with small arms by the whole allied army: the running fire between every round of cannon three times. Two short 6 pounders came from Lier.

MAY 26th BOUWEL CAMP
A foraging party of the artillery and foot ordered to bring in some hay. Left camp at 3 am and returned by 11 am with forage.

The same day at 4 pm a French captain, who was taken up as a spy, was hanged near Fleming's Regiment [36th].

MAY 27th
A foot soldier was hanged for desertion.

[5] Anson defeated the French Fleet off Finisterre, 3 May, 1747.

MAY 28th

A review of eight short six pounders and four regiments of foot; viz: the Old Buffs [3rd], Pulteney's [13th], Wolfe's [8th] and Green Howards [19th]. A spark of fire happening to fall in the haversack of powder, blew up and dangerously wounded the man that carried the haversack, wounded a bombardier and a Lieutenant of the artillery. It's thought the two latter will recover. All passed by the Duke, and he took particular notice of them.

MAY 31st

The Duke came to see us fire at a target: brought two pieces of cannon, and the Austrians likewise brought 2 pieces; fixed the cannon about eight hundred yards from the target. The English knocked the target down the second fire; the Austrians fired but did not come up to us in firing. We likewise fired grapeshot. Both parties fired in a good line. Fired a short 6-pounder ten times in a minute. The Duke and the Prince of Hesse seemed to be very well pleased with the performance.

JUNE 6th BOUWEL CAMP

An alarm in the morning and had all our tents struck by 4 am, but there being a sort of a stand we lay on our arms until 12. The Adjutant came with orders from the Duke to pitch our tents again; the foot marched about 8 miles before the orders came: it seems it was a false alarm.

JUNE 13th

Orders came for the march and we were all ready by 6 am. Marched until 7 pm, pitched our tents; marched about 15 miles.

JUNE 14th

At 6 am marched and came to a halt at 2 pm and pitched our tents, near a town called Diest; name of the camp Meldert.

JUNE 16th

At 6 pm struck our tents and lay on our arms all that night. Expecting to march every minute.

JUNE 17th

Marched about 8 am; a very pleasant part of the country; came to a halt at 6 pm in a large open plain, within 18 miles of Maastricht, the name of the camp Zonhofen.

JUNE 19th

Marched by 4 am and came to our quarters by 4 pm within 6 miles of Maastricht, marched about 12 miles.

JUNE 20th BATTLE MAASTRICHT

Marched by 3 am and left Maastricht 1 mile to the left. About 12 noon the French hussars attacked our hussars on a hill whereon proceeded a smart engagement. In a little time we made them retreat into a village where they had a battery of 5 or 6 guns, but the English immediately brought up to the top of the hill six 6-pounders: a great many shots were fired on both sides. We blew up one of their batteries with a shell and killed a great many of them, though there was scarce any such thing as seeing them, by reason the village was so thick with trees. They killed but two of our men that evening; 1 bombardier and 1 mattross. It rained so prodigious hard that at last both parties left off firing. In the meantime we detached two pieces of cannon to every regiment as far as they would allow of by number. They were short sixes and long 3-pounders. Drew the rest of the heavy cannon into the park and in the night erected batteries for our 12 and 9-pounders facing the village, and prepared ourselves in readiness for an engagement the next day. Lay on our arms all that night in the open field. Continued raining all night. Nothing to be got to eat. Prince of Waldeck commanded the Dutch, Marshall Bathiany the Austrians, and Bavarians.

SUNDAY JUNE 21st BATTLE MAASTRICHT PLAIN[6]

The English began cannonading from our batteries that were erected in the night. We began about 5 am. The French began about 6 am, and continued cannonading until 8.30 am; then the French advanced; accordingly the English, Hanoverians and Hessians advanced with two pieces of cannon with every regiment. Advanced and fired at one another for three hours and a half, as fast as we could load. At 11.30 am they at last retreated, we following with loud hurrahs, but the Dutch horse gave way and the Austrians never coming to back us, and a large body of both horse and foot coming from the right to the assistance of the French and, as they say, the French King coming up along with them inspired them with new life and courage which caused them

---

[6] Commonly known as the Battle of Laufeld or Val.

immediately to turn and advance on us most furiously; and they really behaved very well, though we cut them down with grapeshot from our batteries of 12-pounders yet they did not seem to mind it, but filled up their intervals that we made with grapeshot as they advanced. Being overpowered we were at last obliged to retreat something faster than we advanced and in our retreating we left nine 3-pounders, six short 6-pounders, one long 6-pounder with three colours and a kettle drum.[7]

Our army lost about six thousand, the French ten thousand men; the Hanoverians lost six pieces of cannon. As to the loss of men on both sides I cannot tell as yet. Sir John Ligonier was taken prisoner and several officers of distinction. We lost more of the artillery people that day than ever was known at any battle before, but if the Dutch had done their duty and the Austrians had come in to back us we should certainly have won the day, but was obliged to retreat as far as Maastricht and lay on our arms that night. If it had not been for the town that covered our retreat, we should certainly have been all taken prisoner. This battle was on the Plains of Maastricht, near Wyk. This was called the Battle of Val, or Laffelt; French commander Marshall General of France Count Saxe.

JUNE 22nd
Crossed the Meuse over our pontoon bridge that was made on the day before by the pontoon men and marched about 3 miles at the other side of Maastricht. Pitched our tents and rested very well that night.

JUNE 23rd
A detachment of Dragoons and one Colonel marched from here with 21 waggons to a place called the Bush to get powder and stores where our artillery had winter quarters last year (Bois Le Duc).

JUNE 28th
Richolt Camp: marched by 10 am about 4 miles to the right and pitched our tents on a hill facing the French. They on one side of the water and we on the other side in sight of one another.

JULY 8th
The English began to make fresh works round that part of Maastricht where the French lay to keep them from laying siege to that part of the town, we having drafts detached from the artillery and a quantity of

[7] These were the guns detached to Infantry.

men from each regiment of foot and our hussars to keep the French from advancing towards the breastworks.

July 31st
Almost 10 pm there fell a prodigious quantity of white flies that had light in them; they stuck against the tents and fell down dead. The next morning we could take up pecks of them. They had a long white body with white wings.

August 5th
Came here sixteen brass guns, twelve of them short 6-pounders and four 10-pounders.

August 8th
Marched by 8 am 7 miles to the left: about 12 pitched our tents; the Austrians lay on the ground that we came off, the Hessians next, the Hanoverians next and the English next to them. This camp was called Richel.

August 11th Richel Camp
Orders for two 3-pounders, ammunition and men to the river of Meuse to keep the French from making any attempt to cross and began to prepare making a fascine battery in the night, they lying so nigh they could see what was done by day and almost hear what was said. Command of 4 men sent out of every regiment to work in the night at the battery until it was finished: a fresh relief sent every two days. At the same time we were preparing the same works at a place called Visé near the waterside where we had a breastwork for three guns: a two days' command – the above place where we were making the battery was called Argenta and the other place called Visé.

August 19th
A command of 4 short sixes, men and ammunition marched to a place called Lightingburgh; there was a battery prepared for several guns which was made by the foot the time we lay near that place.

August 25th
A command of four short sixes and three long with men and ammunition ordered to march that night to the other four guns at Lightingburgh near Maastricht which made eleven guns: it is about 17 miles from our camp.

AUGUST 29th RICHEL CAMP

A detachment of foot to number 70 to 80 drafted to us and is to do the duty of mattrosses and to receive pay as such.

AUGUST 30th

The men that were drafted to us yesterday were all sent to Bergen-op-Zoom with Lieutenant Abraham Tovey and two bombardiers.

SEPTEMBER 1st

At 1 am sent a command to relieve the men belonging to the eleven guns that lay at the lines of Lightingburgh which was to be relieved every eight days.

SEPTEMBER 3rd

A party of Hussars had an engagement with a French regiment about 8 miles to the right of our camp, took some of the officers prisoner and a stand of Colours with a great many men and women and 30 or 40 horses which marched by our camp at 11 am.

SEPTEMBER 4th

About 7 pm three officers deserted from the French. They came to the waterside in pretence of watering their horses and swam across the Meuse. There were several shots fired at them from the guard and sentries belonging to the French; they got clear over and were brought to the Duke's quarters: they crossed the water near a place called Argenta.

SEPTEMBER 6th RICHEL CAMP

Arrived here the last of the five Hanoverian regiments and pitched their tents to the right of us. Likewise 17 pieces of cannon: 192 gunners which they call constables, 84 waggons with ammunition and stores.

SEPTEMBER 7th

We receive various news about Bergen-op-Zoom being taken by the French. Sometimes it is taken and sometimes it is not.

SEPTEMBER 13th

An account came that the French had taken Bergen-op-Zoom and that the English and Dutch had got in to the French trenches and had surrounded them: as to the veracity of it I cannot tell – we have an

epidemical disorder throughout all our Allied Army which is the
Bloody Flux; carries several off in a day; they say the French has the
same Distemper but more violent.

SEPTEMBER 14th
The 4 regiments of Hessian Horse and the 6 regiments of Hessian Foot
marched from here, likewise several regiments of Hanoverian marched
in the evening; the French had a *feu de joie* and fired several pieces of
cannon and a running fire by the Foot. They seem still to have a great
number of forces in the field as appeared by the fire.

SEPTEMBER 19th RICHEL CAMP
The French had another rejoicing which was near us. They fired as
before: the rejoicing was on account of the taking of Bergen-op-Zoom
which we hear they took on 5th instant.

SEPTEMBER 21st
The French marched from their camp as supposed for winter quarters;
they set their huts on fire, likewise part of their works.

OCTOBER 3rd
All the English, both horse and foot, likewise the train, marched about
3 miles beyond Maastricht and pitched our tents about 5 pm. This camp
was called Hoitchat. The Hanoverians had orders to march the 5
instant.

OCTOBER 4th
The twelve-pounders, nines and sixes were sent to Maastricht in order
to be embarked on bow bilanders for to sail for the Bush.

OCTOBER 6th
Marched by 8 am and came to camp by 6 pm: marched 20 miles.

OCTOBER 8th EINDHOVEN CAMP
Marched by 8 am and pitched our tents by 3 pm within one mile of
Eindhoven where the Duke took up his quarters: marched about 12
miles.

OCTOBER 9th
The Duke left Eindhoven by 7 am and its thought went for the Hague.

OCTOBER 10th

Marched by 7 am and went through Eindhoven; about 2 pm marched through Oirschot and at 6 pm pitched our tents within 2 miles of Oosterwyck and 9 miles from the Bush. Marched about 10 miles.

OCTOBER 12th

About 12 noon all the carriages belonging to the 12, 9 and 6-pounders with a detachment of men went for the guns to the Bush.

OCTOBER 14th

Set out about 7 am and marched through Oosterwyck and about 12 noon marched through Tilburg: about 4 pm pitched our tents within 6 miles of Breda.

OCTOBER 15th

Marched by 8 am and came to camp by 2 pm and pitched our tents 3 miles beyond Breda where we are designed to have Winter Quarters.

OCTOBER 16th BREDA CAMP

General Howard's regiment marched by us and pitched their tents next to the artillery.

OCTOBER 22nd

Marched from here General Cope's regiment of dragoons and marched by us a regiment of Dutch soldiers that came from Breda – came here General Wolfe's regiment and the second battalion of Highlanders belonging to Lord Loudoun[8] pitched their tents half a mile from the artillery.

OCTOBER 27th

Marched from here about 9 am the train of artillery and came to Breda about 10.30 am and got quarters by 12 noon. The same time came from camp two regiments of English foot and had quarters in Breda.

[8] Meaning second to Lord John Murray's 42nd Regt. John Campbell, Earl of Loudoun, had raised a Regiment during the '45 and it was disbanded at the peace of 1748. This is a unique reference to it serving in Holland as a second battalion of Highlanders (see below).

OCTOBER 29th
Came in four more regiments of English foot; the artillery employed in unloading the stores and taking the guns off the carriages.

OCTOBER 30th
Came in four more regiments of English foot, the artillery employed in proving the guns with water.

OCTOBER 31st
Came in two more English regiments; the Dutch regiment marched out to make room for the English; about 3 pm arrived the Duke of Cumberland and took his quarters at the Prince of Orange's house.

NOVEMBER 3rd
Came here Prince Wolfenbuttel to visit the Duke. Took up his lodging there; the artillery people employed in washing the carriages and putting them into stores.

NOVEMBER 4th
The Duke set out from here in order to go for England.

NOVEMBER 5th
Left out of the stores all the 3-pounders and the carriages belonging to them, likewise the other guns that were not serviceable in order to be sent to England.

NOVEMBER 7th
At 11 am all the English soldiers, likewise the artillery people were under arms on the parade and took an oath at the same time: held the two first fingers of their right hand while the oath was read which was that we were to aid and assist the inhabitants and not to wrong or defraud them in case they should be invaded. The oath was taken before my Lord Albemarle[9] and the Governor of the town.

BREDA
The pontoon boats came in about 12 noon and it seems the French have sent a summons to this town.

[9] William Anne 2nd Earl, Acting C-in-C in Cumberland's absence.

November 8th

Order for all the soldiers to appear clean on the Parade in order to go to church at 10.30 am. Marched all to the "great church". Prayers and sermon were read by one of our English ministers.

November 10th Breda

Colonel Belford and several more officers of the artillery with other officers set out from here in order to proceed to England.

November 11th

Major Williamson set out from here to go to England, left Captain Chalmers to command the 5 companies of artillery.

November 12th

Drafted some of the artillery men that were at Bergen-op-Zoom to the 5 companies of artillery. [These had come out from Woolwich to help at Bergen]

November 13th

The artillery people employed in putting the damaged guns and carriages on board the bilanders in order to sail for England.

November 16th

A draft of artillery marched from here in order to embark on board some of the transports that lay near Williamstadt: it's thought they are going on some expedition.[10]

November 28th

The five companies of artillery were detached to the several works round the ramparts to be ready to repair to their batteries at a moments warning. It's thought the French are on their march in order to lay siege to this town.

November 30th

The artillery unloaded a bilander that came from port with 7 brass six-pounders.

---

[10] Possibly for the recapture of Madras under Admiral Boscawen.

DECEMBER 1st

Unloaded a bilander with the carriages for the above guns with stores ammunition and deals for the use of our carriages and pontoon boats.

FEBRUARY 29th 1748

Major Williamson arrived here from England. Nothing happening material from November 30th.[11]

MARCH 5th

About 700 or 800 French prisoners that were taken at Bergen-op-Zoom by the Dutch and Austrians came here under a strong guard.

MARCH 6th

Four regiments marched from here in order to proceed towards Maastricht for it's thought the French are going to lay siege to it. These several days past the artillery employed in getting ready the guns and stores in order for the next campaign.

MARCH 25th BREDA

Colonel Belford arrived here from England.

MARCH 26th

Recruits for the artillery came here from England and the artillery clothing with two trumpeters in order to join with the kettle drums. The clothing was sent back to the Bush by water and a guard of the artillery sent along with the clothing.

MARCH 28th

The Duke of Cumberland arrived here: the Dutch fired the guns on the ramparts to salute him; the same day the artillery was detached to their guns.

MARCH 29th

The Duke left Breda. A salute of guns was fired. The same day the recruits belonging to the artillery were ordered to their respective companies.

---

[11] Major Williamson, who had served in Minorca, was a technical expert and wrote a manual on gunnery, after tests in Port Mahon. He became a Major-General.

MARCH 30th

Orders for all to be in readiness to march next morning by 7 am through Bush port. Marched about 15 miles, the foot pitched their tents about 4 miles beyond Tilburg: the artillery lay in barns by reason their tents were not come from the Bush. Fired our evening gun about 6.30 pm.

MARCH 31st

Marched by 7 am and about 12 noon came to Oosterwyck and at 4 pm came to our ground about 5 miles from the Bush. Marched about 14 miles. The artillery lay in barns, the foot pitched their tents about 2 miles from the artillery; a command from the artillery went to the Bush in order to guard our clothing and stores that were expected here.

APRIL 1st

Came from the Bush three 9-pounders and two long sixes with several stores and the artillery's clothing. The artillery gave in their firelocks and received carbines in their stead.

APRIL 2nd

Set out at 9 am and marched through moors all day. Came to our ground about 9 pm near a village called Uden. Marched 16 miles. Colonel Belford was at the ground before us with twenty-six short 6-pounders, ammunition and stores. The artillery pitched their new tents.

APRIL 3rd

Marched over a common 7 miles long, came to our ground at 2 pm: marched 9 miles.

APRIL 4th

The gunners and mattrosses had their new clothes given.

APRIL 5th

Marched through Boxmeer 12 miles from the place we left at 9 am. Came to our ground; marched 15 miles.

APRIL 6th

Crossed the Meuse over a Boated Bridge and marched through Venloo and encamped a mile and a half from Venloo. Marched 15 miles.

April 8th Hellingrook Camp

Set out at 8 am and at 9 am marched through a village where the Duke had his quarters. Marched about 3 miles further and pitched our tents. Here we found the other regiments. This Camp was called Hellingrook within 4 miles of a town called Roermond and within 30 miles of Maastricht. About two days after we lay here we could hear the guns from Maastricht, the French having begun to invest that place and preparing for a siege.

April 12th

Two short sixes were sent to every foot regiment which lay in the field with a detachment of artillery to every two guns with one officer. We had in the field at that time 15 foot regiments and 5 of horse viz; Duke's dragoons, Scots Greys, Lord Rothes', Sir Robert Rich's and General Cope's; foot viz: three battalions of Foot Guards, Lord Harry Beauclerk's, which is the young Buffs, Lord George Sackville's, Lord Rothes', Lord Loudoun's and Lord John Murray's, Highland Watch, General Fleming's, General Wolfe's, General Campbell's Scotch Fusiliers, General Huske's Welsh Fusiliers, General Howard's, General St Clair's Royal Scotch and Colonel Conway's.[12]

April 19th Hellingrook Camp

The Pontoons marched from here with orders to make bridges about two miles beyond Roermond.

April 21st

The Duke and several officers passed through the lines of the regiments and as he passed by every regiment turned out at the front of their lines.

April 29th

A cessation of arms was given out in orders. The Duke at the same time gave orders that the troops should go under the same discipline as usual.

[12] The Duke of Cumberland's Light Dragoons were mainly Kingston's Light Horse raised for the '45 re-enlisted. They were to be disbanded in 1748/9. The reference to Lord Rothes being Colonel of a Regiment of Foot, as well as Cavalry, appears to be an error and should be Douglas. Loudoun and Murray are here credited with being Colonels of a Battalion of the Black or Highland Watch (Black Watch). The Young Buffs were the 31st Foot, Fleming's the 36th Foot, Sackville's the 20th.

MAY 1st

Orders to strike our tents. Marched by 9 am, crossed over the three bridges that was made on lighters: one for the infantry, one for the cavalry and one for the train of artillery. They were one mile from Roermond. Marched about 3 miles further and pitched our tents in an open cornfield. The name of this camp Keysersbosch.

MAY 3rd

Marched by 7 am the front came to camp by 4 pm but the rear of the train did not arrive at camp until 10 am the next morning, the roads being so excessive bad. Marched 12 miles: name of the camp, Rewlet by a town called Weert.

MAY 9th

The infantry marched by 7 pm. The train guard was relieved by Pulteney's regiment who were to march with the artillery and to mount guard over the guns and stores. Colonel Belford sent a great many Boors with a detachment of the artillery to make fascines to mend the roads we were to march along.

MAY 10th

The artillery marched by 6 am. About 11 am marched through Boxtel which was to the left of the Austrians' camp. Came to our ground about 3 pm and encamped about 2 miles from the Bush and near a village called Vught which was the name of the camp.

MAY 11th NESSELROY CAMP

Marched by 8 am. About 11 am marched through Bush. At 3 pm came to our ground, encamped on an open moor. 10 miles from the Bush of Brabant where was joined all the English army and four more regiments that lay at Breda with three more that came from England.

MAY 12th NESSELROY CAMP

The artillery had their new hats and shoes given them. Sent six more short sixes to the three regiments: two to each regiment with a detachment to man them.

MAY 17th

Lines were made about half a mile from the Duke's quarters for all the foot, horse and artillery in order to be reviewed by the King, as he is daily expected.[13]

MAY 21st
Sir John Ligonier reviewed the artillery: he being made Lieutenant-General in the room of General Wade, left a present of 50 ducats for their behaviour.[14]

MAY 22nd
The Duke was reviewing some of the foot regiments and the gunner in ramming up the charge of one of the short sixes, it went off and blew off the arm that rammed home and the end of the ramrod struck a foot soldier in the head and killed him on the spot and wounded several others.

MAY 24th NESSELROY CAMP
The artillery was all under arms to be reviewed by the Duke at 4 pm. An express arrived that the Duke could not come that evening.

MAY 26th
The artillery all under arms, about 5 pm the Duke came with a great many general officers and Sir John Ligonier: the word of command given by the Major; the Duke seemed to be very much pleased with our behaviour.

JUNE 11th
All the regiments were under arms by 4 pm for a *feu de joie*, it being the King's succession to the Crown. There were 22 regiments [battalions?] of English infantry and 5 of cavalry and the heavy train which was 6 twelve-pounders, 6 nine-pounders and 14 long sixes. The Hanoverians that were under arms were 21 regiments of infantry and 10 of horse: they were drawn up in two lines, the English and Hanoverian horse at the right of the first and second line; and the Hanoverian infantry at the left of the first and second line; the front line reached about $3\frac{1}{2}$ miles, as likewise did the second. The English train was drawn up in the centre of the rear line.[15] The Duke took his

[13] Actually King George II went direct to Hanover.

[14] A customary present to the Royal Artillery.

[15] This was unusual – from an order of 1756 the guns always took the right of the dismounted line.

post between the Hanoverians and the English. At sunset the train fired and then they began at the right of the front line with a running fire and so went back in the rear to the right: then the artillery fired 50 rounds or more and the foot took it up before with a running fire which was performed three times, with 3 huzzahs up and down the line in the manner of the running fire, and then ordered to march to our camps which we arrived at by 9 pm.

SUNDAY JUNE 19th NESSELROY CAMP
The Duke of Newcastle arrived here with a great retinue.[16]

MONDAY JUNE 26th
The Dukes of Cumberland and Newcastle with several other Lords and Generals passed through the front and rear of our lines in order to review the foot and horse.

JUNE 29th
The English cavalry was reviewed by the Duke with a sham fight, where they charged one another several times and then marched in order by the Duke: they made a very handsome appearance.

JULY 1st GAFFEN CANTONMENTS
The artillery marched from camp by 4 am and came to their cantonment by 10 am to a straggling village called Gaffen. Had their quarters in barns and Johnson's regiment [33rd] lay about two miles from us at a place called Newland: which is the regiment that is to do duty over the guns. Fixed our park about one mile from Gaffen and mounted a guard of artillery there.

JULY 3rd
Divine Service performed by Dr Barton, Chaplain to the Artillery, in Gaffen Church.

JULY 15th
Five Pontoon boats went from here in order to make a bridge over the river for the soldiers to cross and exercise in a large meadow.

[16] He had, as Secretary of State, come over with the King to Hanover.

AUGUST 4th GAFFEN

A general sickness through all the English regiments: taken with a pain in the head, fever and ague. About $\frac{3}{4}$ of the regiments had it and a great number died especially those which lay on the low ground: the only remedy was setons[17] in the neck and drinking the water after it was boiled.

SEPTEMBER 26th

The horses from the artillery sent to bring home the 44 short sixes from the English foot regiments.

OCTOBER 1st

The short sixes arrived with a guard of 100 men: in about 1 hour the guard returned to their regiments.

OCTOBER 17th

About 60 of the worst men belonging to the artillery were sent home to England in order to be discharged.

OCTOBER 20th

The artillery men were ordered down to the park to turn the cannon that the horses should take them off with more ease.

OCTOBER 21st

A detachment of 100 artillery with the miners, one kettle drummer and 2 trumpeters and 2 drummers and all the 12 pounders, nines and long sixes with their ammunition sent to the Bush to be put on board.

OCTOBER 22nd

A command of 36 men with one drummer marched from here by 6 am with all the short sixes to the Bush: was received by the other command at the gate going into the Bush; they doing the work at the Quay, which was dismantling the guns and stowing them on board the bilanders with their stores and the command of 36 men returned by 2 pm.

---

[17] A means of extruding and draining pus with a tight dressing.

OCTOBER 26th

A command of 12 men with the 2 howitzers, spare waggons and ammunition marched from here by 7 am and were received by the command that worked at the Bush. The command of 12 men returned by 2 pm.

OCTOBER 29th

All the artillery marched from Gaffen by 6 am. Marched through the Bush with beat of drum and embarked on board the bilanders by 11 am. Weighed anchor for 12 and came to Crevecour by 2 pm. It is a small garrison town to preserve the sluices. Came to anchor by 9 pm.

OCTOBER 30th

Weighed anchor by 7 am. Sailed by a garrison town called Werkendam about 9 am and at 10 am passed another garrison town called Genderen and about 1 pm landed at Dort [Dordrecht], a large well built town and very clean.

OCTOBER 31st DORT [DORDRECHT]

The artillery employed in unloading the bilanders and putting them in the transports with all expedition.

NOVEMBER 2nd/3rd

The artillery was employed in the same work and getting the officers baggage on board.

NOVEMBER 4th

Three companies of the Royal Artillery embarked on board the three transports for England and set sail by 2 pm. The wind at east about 4 pm struck on the sands and cast anchor.

NOVEMBER 5th

Sailed by 6 am and at 6 pm cast anchor near Williamstadt.

NOVEMBER 6th

Weighed anchor at 2 am, came in sight of Helvoetsluys and at 5 pm cast anchor near Helvoetsluys where Admiral Anson was with 8 men of war and 5 yachts with the King's Yacht waiting His Majesty's return from Hanover.

NOVEMBER 8th

The wind continuing foul sailed into Helvoetsluys harbour at 12 noon. About 40 sail of transports passed us going for Williamstadt in order to embark the soldiers to England.

NOVEMBER 9th HELVOETSLUYS

Passed by us the other two companies of artillery that was left at Dort and immediately we weighed anchor and sailed with a brisk wind; lay to at night: at 3 am sailed.

NOVEMBER 10th

Sailed slowly until 10 am. Came in sight of England about 11 am. Passed by Harwich and at 6 pm anchored in the Swine within two leagues of the Nore.

NOVEMBER 11th

Weighed anchor and at 9 am passed by the Nore and at 7 pm anchored near Sheerness. At night weighed and sailed until 2 the next morning and anchored in the Hope within 3 miles of Tilbury Fort almost opposite Gravesend.

NOVEMBER 12th

Weighed anchor and left the Hope at 9 am. At 10 am sailed by Gravesend, at 2 pm the tide being done, anchored within 3 miles of Woolwich.

NOVEMBER 18th

Weighed anchor by 10 am and towed the ships, there being scarce any wind and got safe to Woolwich by 3 pm, being absent from Woolwich 2 years 6 months and 10 days.

SCOTLAND

1749–1751

NARRATIVE

IT IS REMARKABLE that, having survived the expedition to L'Orient and two seasons campaigning in the Low Countries, James Wood still remained a volunteer working with John Chalmers, whose company remained at Woolwich until the end of 1749. It seems to show considerable irregularity of organization. There was no doubt that Cumberland's experience in the Low Countries moved him to try and improve the organization and training at Woolwich which still left a good deal to be desired after the reforms of 1744. A paper of 1748 proposing reforms at the RMA, "so as to supply a sufficient number of young gentlemen to be compleat officers and perfect engineers", is in the Cumberland papers at Windsor. A sub-governor commandant was to be appointed and the subaltern of the cadet company was to be given the local rank of Captain to become assistant to the commandant. Despite the new orders promulgated through Sir John Ligonier, Lieutenant-General of the Ordnance, things were little better by 1750, when Müller, the German-born professor and chief instructor, reported to the Adjutant General that "the cadets come and go as they please in complete frustration of orders. They work or are idle without the officers taking any notice of it – the captain/lieutenant is never there – I have not been able to make one capable of surveying." Müller concluded by stating that he would give up the job if he could find anything better to do – which of course he did not.

Another sidelight on artillery appointments at this date can be gleaned from a letter from James Wolfe to his mother. "Nobody, I believe, doubts that HRH disposes of all employments in the Corps of Artillery as much as if he was Grand Master [of the Ordnance] and, as he has their well being vastly at heart, he takes proper pains to place proper people to the vacancies that men of abilities may appear among them." It is not perhaps surprising therefore that the next section of Wood's diary gives a unique insight into the employment of Field Artillery in

Scotland in the aftermath of Culloden. In that battle Major Belford and his ten pieces of light field artillery deployed in pairs between front line battalions played a decisive role. He and his men then departed for service in the low countries in 1747 and 1748 as Wood describes. But an artillery company commanded by Captain Thomas Flight took over from Belford in Scotland, mustering at Fort Augustus, and set up its headquarters in Perth in July, 1746. According to the muster rolls Flight's company was disbanded in February 1749 before it was relieved.

According to Wood's account it was not until nearly a year later that Chalmers' company assumed the field artillery task in Scotland, working with infantry battalions at Fort William, Fort Augustus, Inverness, Perth and Edinburgh. We do not know how many guns there were in support of the various garrisons which probably retained their own master gunners and gunners under the Fort Major, looking after the stores and weapons. The artillery reliefs were certainly not punctually carried out and infantrymen were expected to serve the guns if necessary.

The totally unexpected circumstance is that Chalmers' company carried out its tour in Scotland by march route. After the experience of sea transport in 1746 it seems extraordinary that the Ordnance Board did not move the personnel by sea from the Thames to Leith. In his account Wood describes the stages of the march but gives us no inkling as to where the men put up – probably in inns – along the great north road and commits nothing to paper regarding food, weather and company. He certainly did not regard the march as unusual – Flight's men had marched – and he makes no reference to scenery or local inhabitants. Nor do we have any description of what he and his colleagues actually did in Scotland. It was not even a ground for complaint that they set out on Christmas Eve!

From instructions given to General Churchill, the GOC in C in Scotland, we know that for the seven infantry battalions in Scotland it was a busy time. In summer they carried out a considerable road building programme, as well as manning small and very isolated posts all over the Highlands to enforce the laws against the wearing of tartan plaids and the carrying of arms by the Highland clans.

It is of particular interest that, despite what Muller told Cumberland about the lack of surveyors from the RMA, one of the officers in Wood's company carried out surveying. Lieutenant George Campbell was put to work to map the country around Braemar and on the Findhorn in order to help the engineers complete the great Highland Survey, and to trace the best line for the roads being constructed by the infantry working parties with expert assistance from locally recruited artisans. It seems that no gunners or mattrosses were sent on these duties, for which the infantry soldiers received 8d a day additional pay, compared with a pay rate of 6d a day for smiths and carpenters, and 2d a day for wallers, pavers and miners. Masons under contract received only 1d a day. All of which goes to show that despite much that has been said to the contrary, the British regular soldier in the 18th century was comparatively well paid.

During the period Wood was in Scotland General Churchill's task was to assist Colonel David Watson and Major Caulfield complete roads from Braemar to Blair Atholl, Dumbarton to Inveraray, from Fort William to Stirling via Tyndrum and from Fort Augustus to Bernera. Something like £15,000 was allowed for expenditure over the three years 1749–1751! Hard by Inverness work was proceeding throughout the period on the building of Fort George at Ardiseer, according to the plans of Colonel Skinner. Wood may himself have had an uneventful time but for the army as a whole they were busy years in opening up the Highlands and consolidating the defences of the Highland line so that artillery pieces could be moved more rapidly overland in all weathers. It will not be missed that as in the case of the Chalmers/Flight relief the relief Pattison/Chalmers was not as tidy as one would have wished. The two companies actually passed in Berwick so that, for a time, once more the infantry crewed the guns. It is a pity that no references to the number and types of weapon can be found. Were they the very same pieces that Belford had fired so effectively at Culloden, $1\frac{1}{2}$ and 6 pounders? It seems somewhat unlikely, knowing the increases made in the artillery train since that date. Wood made considerable note of artillery matters in Holland but not a single observation escapes him in Scotland.

SCOTLAND 1748

DECEMBER 24th
Captain Chalmers' Company was ordered to march for Scotland to take the command there and about 6 am marched from Woolwich; about 9 am came to London and marched to Highgate where we had quarters that night.

DECEMBER 29th
Set out by 4 am with Captain Lieutenant Farquharson and Lieutenant Campbell. Marched by 12 noon to St Albans where we had quarters: nothing material happening from London to Edinburgh but lived jovial all along the road, it being Christmas time.

FEBRUARY 3rd
Arrived at Edinburgh, having been 41 days on our march from Woolwich. Captain Chalmers, Lieutenant McCulloch and 16 men remained at Edinburgh, the remainder marched to Perth which is 28 miles from Dundee.

FEBRUARY 6th PERTH
A command of artillery marched from here to relieve the other command at Inverness which was to be relieved every year.

FEBRUARY 8th 1749 SCOTLAND
Marched from Perth another command to relieve the artillery command at Fort William.

MAY 6th
A command of artillery sent to Edinburgh with 4 waggons for some powder. The command returned on 10th.

MAY 10th

The command was relieved at Edinburgh by a command of artillery from Perth. Nothing material happened until September 1751 when an order came to Perth for the command of Artillery that was at Inverness, Fort Augustus and Fort William to repair to Perth and to be relieved by the Foot that did duty there.

SEPTEMBER 28th [1751]

All the artillery at Perth arrived at Leith within one mile of Edinburgh. The same afternoon the command of artillery at Edinburgh marched down to Leith to join them in order for the company of artillery to march for Woolwich.

SEPTEMBER 30th LEITH, EDINBURGH

The whole company of artillery marched from Leith in the shire of Midlothian by 7 am to Musselburgh.

From Leith to Musselburgh	4 miles	Computed 12 miles
From Musselburgh to Tranent	3 miles	
From Tranent to Haddington, East Lothian	5 miles	

OCTOBER 1st

From Haddington to East Linton Brigg	4 miles	Computed 16 miles
From Linton Brigg to Broxburn	4 miles	
From Broxburn to Old Cambus – Shire of Berwick	8 miles	

OCTOBER 2nd

From Old Cambus to Eaton	10	17 Measured miles
From Eaton to Berwick – Shire of Berwick	7	

OCTOBER 3rd

Left Captain Pattison's company of artillery where we met at Berwick on their march to Scotland in order to take the command in the room of Captain Chalmers.

From Berwick to Fenwick	$11\frac{1}{2}$	$15\frac{1}{2}$ Measured miles
From Fenwick to Belford	4	

OCTOBER 4th
From Belford to Charlton	9	}	14½
From Charlton to Alnwick	5½		Measured miles

OCTOBER 5th
From Alnwick to Felton	9	}	19
From Felton to Morpeth	10		Measured miles

OCTOBER 7th 1751
From Morpeth to Stanington	5	}	15
From Stanington to Newcastle on Tyne in the Bishopric of Durham	10		

OCTOBER 8th
From Newcastle to Chester Le Street	9	}	15
From Chester Le Street to Durham	6		

OCTOBER 9th
From Durham to Ferry Hill	6½	}	18
From Ferry Hill to Aycliffe	6½		
From Aycliffe to Darlington, Durham	5		

OCTOBER 11th
From Darlington to Croft, Yorkshire	4	}	16
From Croft to Great Smeaton	5		
From Smeaton to Northallerton	7		

OCTOBER 12th
From Northallerton to Newsham	6	}	19
From Newsham to Sand Hutton	2		
From Sand Hutton to Topcliffe	4½		
From Topcliffe to Dishforth	2		
From Dishforth to Boroughbridge County of Yorkshire	4½		

OCTOBER 14th
From Boroughbridge to Walshford	8½	}	12
From Walshford to Weatherby	3½		

October 15th

From Weatherby to Bramham	3	
From Bramham to Aberford	4	16
From Aberford to Brotherton	8	
From Brotherton to Ferry Bridge, Yorkshire	1	

October 16th

From Ferry Bridge to Darrington	$2\frac{1}{2}$	
From Darrington to Westbridge	2	15
From Westbridge to Doncaster, Yorkshire	$10\frac{1}{2}$	

October 17th

From Doncaster to Bawtry, end Yorkshire	$8\frac{1}{2}$	13
From Bawtry to Blyth, Nottinghamshire	$4\frac{1}{2}$	

October 18th

From Blyth to Tuxford, Nottinghamshire	13

October 19th

From Tuxford to Newark upon Trent	13

October 20th

Halted at Newark upon Trent, Nottinghamshire.

October 21st

From Newark to Grantham, Lincolnshire	14

October 22nd

From Grantham to Colsterworth	7	
From Colsterworth to Great Casterton	12	21
From Great Casterton to Stamford, Lincolnshire	2	

October 23rd

From Stamford to Wansford	6	
From Wansford to Sibson	1	
From Sibson to Alwalton	1	14
From Alwalton to Stilton, Lincolnshire	6	

October 24th

From Stilton to Huntington, in the shire of Huntington	12

October 25th

From Huntington to Caxton, Cambridgeshire	9

October 26th

From Caxton to Kneesworth	10	
From Kneesworth to Royston Part in Cambridgeshire, the other part in Hertfordshire	2	12

October 27th

Halted at Royston. The fifth days halt.

October 28th

From Royston to Ware	17

October 29th

From Ware to Hackney	21 TOTAL 106 miles

October 30th

Sent the officers' baggage through London with a command of artillery. The other party of artillery marched from Hackney to Woolwich in Kent which is 8 miles. Being absent the second time two years 10 months and six days. Thirty-one days coming from Scotland to Woolwich, being in miles from Edinburgh to London, by my computation 387 miles.

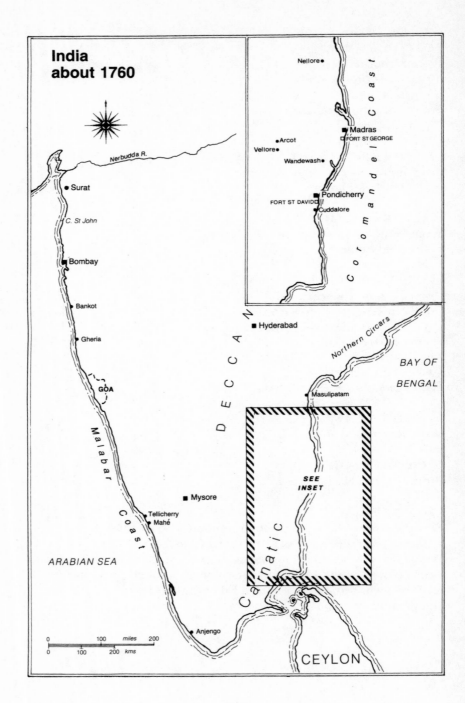

India
about 1760

Nerbudda R.

Surat

C. St John

Bombay

Bankot

Gheria

GOA

DECCAN

Hyderabad

Northern Circars

BAY OF
BENGAL

Masulipatam

Malabar Coast

Mysore

Tellicherry
Mahé

SEE
INSET

ARABIAN SEA

Carnatic

Anjengo

CEYLON

Nellore

Coromandel Coast

Arcot
Vellore
Madras
FORT ST GEORGE

Wandewash

Pondicherry
FORT ST DAVID
Cuddalore

0   100   miles   200
0   100   200   kms

[66]

PASSAGE TO INDIA

1755–1765

NARRATIVE

FIRST THE PORTUGUESE, then the Dutch and finally the French and English sent trading fleets to bring the produce of the Orient to Europe and their transatlantic colonies in exchange for manufactures. The Braganza marriage of Charles II brought not only Tangier but Bombay within the English sphere. Tangier was given up in 1684 but Bombay was handed over to the East India Company which established factories at Gambroon in the Persian Gulf, Surat north of Bombay, Tellicherry on the Malabar coast as well as ports along the Carnatic coast above Madras, northwards into the Bay of Bengal along the Hoogly to Calcutta. The Dutch were largely a successor power to Portugal in Ceylon and the East Indies and the Spaniards were in the Philippines. As an intermediate base the French held Mauritius.

Under the ambitious leadership of Dupleix and Bussy the French Compagnie des Indes attempted to restrict or oust the British footholds in the Carnatic by enlisting the assistance of local rulers and native troops. The breakdown of the Mogul Empire gave them a chance they were not slow to exploit and their capture of Madras from the British after years of skirmishing was a mighty feather in their cap. In 1747 Admiral Boscawen was despatched from England with a force of twelve independent companies, raised in Scotland and Ireland, a company of Royal Artillery and some engineers to aid the East India Company by capturing the French main base at Pondicherry. The attempt failed with considerable loss and it was a sad outcome to the first occasion on which Royal Troops assisted the East India Company. However, at the Peace of Aix-La-Chapelle Madras was returned as a swap for Louisburg on Cape Breton Island. This, however, by no means put an end to the quarrelling either in North America or India. The East India Company was obliged to recruit its forces considerably in the three Presidencies of Bombay, Madras and Bengal, to limit encroachment and consolidate the hinterland of the many factory stations where concessions could be

[67]

negotiated. Bombay, for instance, established its own artillery companies, copied from the British organizations with weapons supplied by the Board of Ordnance and recruited a regiment of European infantry as well as sepoys and topasses[1]. In the Carnatic serious war broke out again and in the Deccan Bussy's intrigues in Hyderabad and Mysore and with Mahratta warrior chiefs produced threats to British interests on the coasts from deep inland. The East India Company in London once more had recourse to the Crown for naval and military aid. In 1754 the Duke of Cumberland obtained a mutiny act for India and detailed the first regular regiment of the British Army, the 39th, to leave Ireland for service in the Carnatic, appointing its British regular colonel as C-in-C. A company of Royal Artillery accompanied the 39th. A squadron of Royal Navy under Admiral Watson sailed with them. The war continuing, early in 1755 it was decided to mount an expedition from the territory of the Bombay Presidency to invade the Deccan. Three companies of Royal Artillery were ordered to Bombay and a fourth to Madras. Colonel Caroline Scott, former ADC to Cumberland, and now chief engineer to the East India Company in Bengal and Madras, was nominated as C-in-C. Lieutenant-Colonel Robert Clive set out from London as second-in-command, with precise instructions from the Directors of the company. Major John Chalmers took command of the three companies RA for Bombay. His subordinate company commanders were Skeddy, Farquharson and Maitland, all in the rank of Captain. James Wood, now an established cadet in the company, which had retrieved its reputation at an inspection by the Duke of Cumberland àt Woolwich in August, 1752, sailed with Major Chalmers for Bombay on the East-Indiaman *Houghton* which also carried Captain Skeddy's company. The company destined for Madras embarked on EIM *Dodington*, forming part of the same convoy as far as the Cape of Good Hope.

James Wood's diary is of particular interest in that it gives us knowledge of the Bombay Presidency at a time when Madras and Bengal drew the limelight. He illustrates garrison life and training as well as giving unique details of operations along the west coast of India during the eight years he served there from 1756 to 1764.

A voyage to India in those days was certainly hazardous. On his first voyage in 1743 Robert Clive had run aground off Brazil and was a year in passage. From Wood's convoy the EIM *Dodington* parted company and it was not known for many months after the arrival of the convoy

---

[1] Sepoy – a native Indian employed as a soldier of the East India Company, whereas a topass strictly means a Portuguese half-breed employed as a soldier.

at Bombay that she had foundered on a rocky islet in the Mozambique channel with the loss of all but 23 souls. Only three men from her company of the Royal Artillery survived to reach India and tell the tale of their terrible privations, courage, enterprise and luck.

The troop-carrying EIM was of 499 registered tons. By keeping the chartered rating below 500 tons the Company, up to 1772, got away with not having a chaplain, it seems! The crew consisted of a Captain, four mates, a surgeon, a purser and 90 crew. The ship mounted 30 guns bought from the Board of Ordnance. The King's Army officers were in cabins each 7 feet by 6 feet and paid the Company passage money at the rate of £135 for a major, £110 for a captain and £95 for a subaltern. Homebound payment was in rupees, 2500, 2000, and 1500 respectively (one pound being equal to about sixteen rupees). The men were accommodated in messes of eight. Civilians and their families went too. There was, of course, considerable jealousy between the military and civilian employees of the East India Company and the addition of the King's Army officers only added to the problems. It was certainly Cumberland's view that the King's commission was superior in the same rank to the East India commission and that the British articles of war and military law should be applied in India for greater efficiency. Wood's diary shows some of the resultant problems but on the whole joint operations were pretty successful, despite the appalling wastage from disease which must have gravely affected operational efficiency and obliged local commanders to take quite unorthodox measures to enlist and commission officers with little or no training. French officers and officials were, by and large, more quarrelsome and less loyal to each other than the British, who enjoyed more continuous naval support than their opponents.

By regular steps of promotion into dead men's shoes Wood was first raised from the rank of cadet in Madagascar and then by three more stages arrived at the rank of Lieutenant RA in Madras in 1762. He outlived almost all the artillery officers he sailed out with to Bombay originally. Not quite all of them had died by the time he returned in 1765. One has equally to remark on the casualty rate among civilians. It is recorded of the British civilian staff of 75 in the Bombay Presidency in 1755 – where, by the way, a writer earned 30 rupees a month as against a 2nd Lieutenant 60 rupees – that only 3 survived to enjoy a fortune in retirement at home; 48 died in India and the remaining 15 retained little more means than to meet their burial expenses in England. "Nabobs" were very few in terms of the numbers serving the Company. Of the rank and file of the regular army who went out few survived the war and those who returned missed professional advancement at home. Several enlisted in the Company's artillery for a bounty.

During the 15,000-mile voyage out Wood must have made close friends with the mates. Otherwise he could hardly have recorded so minutely the daily details of the ship's log. He measures the distance travelled by stages of her passage from the Thames to Madeira; thence by the Cape Verde Islands to Madagascar and on to Bombay. Once out in India he no longer recorded details of navigation, though from Bombay he twice sailed to Madras and back. He came back by Royal Navy ship in 1764/65.

It was probably no surprise that when the convoy reached Bombay Chalmers found all plans had changed. The French and English East India Companies had made peace and Colonel Caroline Scott had died in 1754. Dupleix had been recalled only to be disgraced for his ambition and extravagant conduct. In consequence the Bombay Presidency, Admiral Watson and Robert Clive gave up the march on Hyderabad and substituted a most useful expedition with a Mahratta ally against a nest of pirates not a hundred miles south of Bombay, so as to ensure the safer transit of trade. Wood covers this operation in detail and also describes the Governor of Bombay's use of the King's troops to reestablish order at the Company's factory at Surat. This is notable in the history of the Royal Artillery as the first occasion on which an officer of the Royal Artillery – Maitland – commanded a force of all arms. After success at Surat Wood's company was shipped to the Carnatic coast in time to take part in the operations of Monson and Eyre Coote against the French which culminated in the capture of Pondicherry early in 1761. This was a turning point in the fortunes of war in India.

Wood was also privy to the despatch of the expedition of Admiral Cornish and Colonel Draper with a company of Royal Artillery to capture Manila from the Spanish who came into the Seven Years' War on the side of France in 1761.

The diary has a number of interesting entries which show how far our men in India were kept posted on the main military and political events worldwide which measured the extraordinary progress of the war. It also tells how Royal Artillery officers were commissioned in India from local civilians and officers of other arms to make good deficiencies. A stop was put to the system of volunteers. Out of the remnants of some seven companies of Royal Artillery that had been sent out to serve in the theatre from 1754 less than half-a-dozen officers and about thirty men survived to return with Lieutenant James Wood in 1764. Several men had accepted the option of enlisting in the East India Company's forces, which the King had encouraged. This benefited the Company, saved the Government money and solved the problems of demobilization and pensions.

In July, 1764, Wood and his remnants of Royal Artillery started on their final journey home from Madras on HMS *Weymouth*. It seems that he might have got home earlier, *Weymouth* having been ordered back to Madras from Bombay in May, 1764, and Wood carried back once again around Ceylon, only finally leaving for home in November. When he arrived at the Cape in December, it was to catch a final glimpse of Lord Clive, then on his last tour to India. After touching at St Helena Wood got safely home. The last entry in the diary notes his arrival at Plymouth on 21 June, 1765. Opposite, inside the diary's cover, he inscribed a nominal roll of the officers he went out to India with. This he annotated to show that he outlived them all, the vast majority dying in the course of the diary. From India Barrett and Hetzler alone came home. Despite this he was to find when he reached Woolwich that seventeen officers junior to him regimentally had been promoted over his head. Such was the professional cost of ten years' absence in India.

From many aspects Wood's diary gives us new insight into what John Fortescue in his history has called "the most remarkable development observable during this period in the whole army", namely the growth of the military effectiveness of the Royal Artillery between 1741 and 1760. It is a general observation that little has been done by historians to substantiate in detail. They have largely seen fit to ignore the period between Marlborough and Wellington as of little interest and they have preferred to concentrate on the reputation of the great commanders rather than illuminate with painstaking research, the efficiency, honesty and devotion to duty of the more junior ranks which make at least equally for success in war. Wood's diary helps us to uncover the well-concealed grassroots of our mid-eighteenth century army and furnishes some explanation for its extraordinary success worldwide in the Seven Years War.

WENT TO INDIA – MARCH 1755[2]

Major	John Chalmers	Half Pay, Dead
Captain	Skeddy	Dead
Captain	Maitland	Dead
Captain	Farquharson	Dead
Captain/Lieutenant	Northall	Dead
Captain/Lieutenant	Mason	Dead
First Lieutenant	Jack Tovey	Dead
	Joseph Winter	Dead
	Edward Whitmore	
Second Lieutenant	Sir Charles Chalmers	Dead
	Joseph Barratt	Dead
	Thomas Hussey	Dead
Lieutenant Fireworker	George Campbell	Dead
	Jonathon Lewis	Dead
	Robert Hetzler	Dead
	George Grove	Dead
	John Chalmers	Dead
	John Smith	Dead
	William Corbett	Dead
	Daniel Sweet	Dead
	John Scott	Dead
	James Wood	

[2] The above list is written on the inside end cover of Wood's diary and is annotated in pencil by Wood, one of four survivors of the Royal Artillery officers who sailed with him from Woolwich in 1755. Only Whitmore outlived him.

THE PASSAGE TO INDIA

THURSDAY 20 MARCH 1755 – WOOLWICH
Three companies of the Royal Artillery embarked on board the three
India ships lying at Gravesend, under the command of Major John
Chalmers – Major Chalmers' and Captain Skeddy's companies on board
the *Houghton* commanded by Captain Richard Walpole[3]. Captain
Farquharson's company on board the *Stretham* commanded by Captain
Mason, Captain Maitland's company on board the *Edgecoat*
commanded by Captain Pierce.

FRIDAY 21 MARCH
Unmoored and came to sail at 4 pm, wind s w. At 6.30 pm anchored
in the Hope in 7 fathoms in company with the *Edgecoat* and *Streatham*.

SUNDAY 23 MARCH
At 7 am wind at south, weighed and sailed at 10 am; passed the Nore
light. At 11 am anchored in the Warp in 7 fathoms. Distance from the
Nore light 2 miles.

THURSDAY 27 MARCH
At 1 pm anchored in the Kentish Well in 18 fathoms. At 5 pm came
to sail, wind at w. At 10 pm the North Foreland light s w. At 11 pm
anchored in 16 fathoms. At 6 am weighed and came to sail at 8° the
North Foreland lighthouse. At 10 am worked into Margate road, at
noon Birchington s w b w and the Foreland point s e b e.

---

[3] Richard Walpole's logs for the *Houghton*, 1751–1757, survive. During this time
he made two round trips to China bringing back silks, tea and chinaware. He
and another E.I. ship successfully fought off an attack by French frigates off
the Cape of Good Hope, 1757.

FRIDAY 28 MARCH

At 1.30 pm made sail from Margate road. Worked through the Gulls. Came on board John Sampson, Deal pilot, and our London pilot left us. At 6.30 pm anchored in the Downs in 8 fathoms. Found riding here HMS *Dunkirk* and *Penzance* with several merchant ships to muster the sailors. Came on board Mr Bell. Seven days from Gravesend to the Downs.

SATURDAY 29 MARCH

Mr Bland the purser came on board. The south Foreland bore SWBS, the north Foreland NW and the King's storehouse west – offshore $2\frac{1}{2}$ miles.

SATURDAY 5 APRIL

HMS *Penzance* and most of the merchantmen sailed to the westward.

SUNDAY 6 APRIL

HMS *Torbay* 64 guns came down and anchored here – squalls and rain.

MONDAY 7 APRIL

HMS *Penzance* and all the merchantmen put back; great winds, lowered yards and top masts. Sandown Castle NW.

THURSDAY 10 APRIL

Wind SW. HMS *Nassau*, 70 guns, and *Winchester* 40 guns came down with the *Pelham* EIM, Captain Lindsey, for India with officers and soldiers for the company's service. All anchored here.

FRIDAY 11 APRIL

HMS *Torbay, Dunkirk* and *Penzance* sailed to the westward with all the merchantmen; the wind coming about to the SW obliged the merchantmen to put back. HMS *Prince*, 40 guns, came down and anchored here.

SATURDAY 12 APRIL

The *Dodington* EIM, Captain Sampson, came down bound for Madras in India with 100 of the King's artillery and six officers commanded by Captain/Lieutenant Jones, with about 80 soldiers for the company's service.

FRIDAY 18 APRIL

HMS *Nassau, Prince* and *Cruzer* sloop sailed to the westward with several merchant men.

SUNDAY 20 APRIL

HMS *Barfleur*, 90 guns, and *Lancaster*, 60 guns, anchored here and the next day sailed to the westward.

WEDNESDAY 23 APRIL DOWN CHANNEL

The wind coming east unmoored. At noon set sail in company with the *Pelham, Edgecoat, Stretham* and *Dodington*, and *Houghton* with several merchantmen. Lay in the Downs 26 days.

THURSDAY 24 APRIL DOWN CHANNEL

At 4 pm passed by Dover Castle 4 miles offshore. At sunset the pilot left us. Dungeness lighthouse and the east part of the highlands of Fairlight. Lydchurch, distance from the Ness three leagues[4]. At noon Beachy Head and the body of the highland distance about 5 leagues; latitude observed 50.38. Sailed 35 miles by the log.

FRIDAY 25 APRIL

At sunset Beachy Head northerly about 6 leagues; at noon the extreme of the land at NW to NE. Offshore about 10 leagues, sailed per log 51 miles – 30 fathoms.

SATURDAY 26 APRIL

At 4 pm saw the French shore. At 6 the extreme of the land from SBW to WSW: the westernmost part of which we take to be Cape de la Hague. At 8 am Dunnose distance 8 leagues, sailed by the log 47 miles – 32 fathoms.

SUNDAY 27 APRIL

Peveril point, and Portland NBE, distance 7 or 8 leagues, 35 fathoms. At sunset the island of Alderney SWBW Portland at our side bore EBN about 8 leagues. At noon the Start point WBNBN. Berryhead NBE distance from the Start about 6 leagues. Sailed by the log 45 miles.

---

[4] A League is a distance of 3 nautical miles (3041 fathoms = 6082 yards).

MONDAY 28 APRIL

At 4 pm the Start bore NWBW distance about 4 leagues in 37 fathoms.
At noon Bigbury Church NNW and the westernmost part of Bigbury
Bay NWBN in 39 fathoms offshore 4 leagues, sailed per log 65 miles.

THURSDAY 29 APRIL

At 4 pm the Prawle NE, the Bolt NEBN; the extreme of the land to the
westward NBW: offshore about 4 leagues. At 6 pm the Prawle N$\frac{1}{2}$E the
Bolt tail NBW in 41 fathoms. Take the departure from the Bolt in 50
degrees 08 minutes north 60° with bearings included SW$\frac{1}{4}$W. Distance
83 difference, latitude 56, departure 62 difference longitude 94.
Observed 49°.13′ N. Account, 49°.12′ N. Sailed by the log 85 miles.

MONDAY 5 MAY

John Brown, mattross, died. Committed his body to the deep; prayers
being read by one of the men. At 8 am saw a sail standing to the
westward, bore down to her; found to be a Frenchman from Bordeaux
bound to Cape Breton. Hazy weather. Latitude by account 44.20.
Sailed 131 miles in company with *Pelham* and *Stretham*.

SATURDAY 10 MAY

At daylight saw the Island of Madeira SSW 8 or 9 leagues. The north-
west end of the island, SSE 7 leagues. Saw two sail SE standing to the
eastward. Course SWBW. Latitude by observation 32.43 N; by account
32.47 wind NEBE. Sailed by the log 131 miles – made Madeira in 17
days from the Downs.

SUNDAY 11 MAY

At 7 pm spoke with a brig from London, bound for New York. Took
departure from Madeira latitude 32.23 north, course SW, wind NNE.
Latitude by observation 31.27, by account 31.39 north; sailed 71 miles.

MONDAY 12 MAY

Wind N, course SW. Caught 2 albacore fish. Lat.Obs. 30.49 Acct. 30.54.
Sailed 38 miles.

MONDAY 19 MAY FAIR

At 8 pm saw the island of Sal about 13 leagues distance at 8°; the
extreme of the island from SE to SWBS distance offshore 3 leagues.
At noon the extreme of the island Bonavista SBE to SWBW, the body
SSW distance 2 leagues. Lat. 23.0 by obsn. north, by acct. 16.39 Meridian

distance 3.58 Long. 46.23m; wind NE. Sailed 110 miles. Sailed from Madeira to Saint Iago in 12 days.

TUESDAY 20 MAY FAIR
Course NNW wind NE. At 2 pm the island was about 9 leagues distant. At 6 pm the fore top mast sprung about two foot above the cats. At 9 am spoke with the *Dodington*. The extreme of Bonavista from WBS to NWBW. Distance about 6 leagues. At noon the extreme part of Bonavista NBE distance from the nearest shore 5 leagues. Lat. by obs. 15.53, by acct. 15.40, wind to NNE. Sailed 85 miles course SE.

WEDNESDAY 21 MAY
At sunset the extreme of the Isle of Maya, westerly, distance 3 leagues and the highland of St Iago SBW. At 8 am saw port of St Iago at WSW. Saw a sail for the Isle of Maya at noon. The nearmost part of Praya Bay 1 mile west.

THURSDAY 22 MAY ST IAGO
At 12.30 anchored in Praya road. Lowered the long boat and sent her ashore for water. Found the *Pelham, Stretham* and *Dodington* riding here. At 4 pm a brig from England came in.

FRIDAY 23 MAY ST IAGO CITY AFRICAN ISLAND
The sailors employed mending the foremast and rigging. The inhabitants very poor and mostly naked and a very barren hilly country. About 7 miles up the country the Portuguese Viceroy lives. Called St Iago. Its chief products are salt, goat skins, limes, citrons, oranges, figs, pineapples, coconuts etc. The air reckoned to be unwholesome. Some cotton shrubs grow likewise here. Well stocked with great numbers of monkeys. The cattle very small and poor. The people are very fond of old clothes and will give what the place affords in exchange. Men very ordinary.

SATURDAY 24 MAY ST IAGO
Received on board some livestock and water – very miserable cattle. The most remarkable of the Cape Verde Islands is the Isle de Fuego or Fogo, continually sending up sulphurous fumes and vapours, and sometimes the flames break out in a very terrible manner, which may be seen a great way off as it's a very high island; they have the same religion with those in Portugal.

SUNDAY 25 MAY ST IAGO

Came in the *Edgecoat* EIM (Captain Pierce) – Captain Maitland and all our people in very good health and all very merry except a little quarrelsome. A duel was fought with sword and pistol between Captain/Lieutenant Jones, an artillery officer in the *Dodington*, and another gentleman passenger in the said ship: nothing of consequence happened.

MONDAY 26 MAY ST IAGO

Two snows[5] came in from England and anchored here. Completed our water and got ready for sailing. Five days at St Iago.

TUESDAY 27 MAY

Left in the road the *Edgecoat*, two snows and a brig. At 8 pm weighed and lay to for a Commodore. At 11 made sail in company with the *Pelham,* Captain Lindsay, Commodore, the *Stretham,* Captain Mason, and *Dodington,* Captain Sampson. Latitude of St Iago 15°8' north. Sailed 97 miles.

THURSDAY 29 MAY

Sultry with some squalls of rain in company with the *Pelham* and *Stretham.* Lost sight of the *Dodington.* Lat. by acct. 9.19, by obs. 9.30. Wind SSE Course SBW. Sailed by the log 108 miles.

THURSDAY 5 JUNE

Large swells with squalls from the southward. At 12.30 pm the Commodore made a signal of distress to bring to, having carried away both his top masts. Sent our carpenter with a jib boom on board him. Course S 30 W. Lat. by acct. 3.12; by obs. 2.49. Sailed 40 miles.

SUNDAY 8 JUNE

Lightning bore down to the *Pelham* and took our carpenter on board. Course S°47 W. Lat. by acct. 1.15; by obs. 1.14. Distance by log 64 miles.

---

[5] Snow. Small two-masted sailing vessel but with a topsail mast behind the main mast.

TUESDAY 10 JUNE

Pleasant trade wind. Crossed the Equator – course s 35 w. Distance
70 miles; southing 57 miles; westering 40 miles. Lat. by obs. 0.32s
Lat. by acct. 0.41 s. Distance by log 72 miles.

WEDNESDAY 11 JUNE

Weather as yesterday. Added 12 miles judging the logs distance wrong.
Course s 34 w. Distance 92 miles; southing 76 miles; westering 51 miles.
Lat. by obs. 1.57. Lat by acct. 2.05 south. Meridian distance 0.96 West.
Long, made 0.50 West. Distance by log 80 miles.

THURSDAY 12 JUNE

Squally and rain. Shortened sail for the *Pelham*. Between the Lat. Obs.
and Acct. is judged wrong due to a strong current etc. Courses 21 w
Distance 100 miles; Lat. obs. 3.50; Lat. by acct. 3.30 s. Distance per
log 102 miles.

FRIDAY 13 JUNE FROM ST IAGO

Hazy weather, large swell from the s e; saw a sail to the windward.
Brought to, for the *Stretham* to speak to the sloop. Course s b w. Lat.
5.13 Long. 5.8 s. Distance by log 87 miles.

SATURDAY 14 JUNE

At 8 am Captain Walpole broke the paquet[6] marked n° 12 which was
to be opened in the Lat. 6 South in presence of Charles Haggis and
Richard Dufton, first and second mates. Course s 5 e. Distance 100
miles. Lost sight of *Pelham* and *Stretham*. Lat. by obs. 6.48; Lat. by
acct. 6.50s. Sailed per log 104 miles. Pleasant weather.

TUESDAY 17 JUNE

Fair weather. In company with the *Pelham* and *Stretham*. Long. Made
2.43 of St Iago. Lat. by obs. 8.50 s. Sailed by log 56 miles.

WEDNESDAY 18 JUNE

Cloudy. Large sea from the s e. At 6 am lost sight of the *Pelham* and
Stretham.

---

[6] Presumably his sealed instructions for sailing.

THURSDAY 19 JUNE

Weather as yesterday. The larboard futtock shroud broke; down foretop gallant and yard. Lat. by obs. 12.13s. Sailed by log 135 miles.

SUNDAY 22 JUNE

Variable winds and weather, with some light squalls. Public prayers read by Captain Walpole. Course s distance 113 miles. Southing 113 miles. Lat. by obs. 18.13; Lat. per acct. 18.13s. Sailed per log 113 miles.

TUESDAY 24 JUNE

Variable weather with a pleasant trade wind. Looked out all night for the Island of Trinidada[7] but saw nothing of it. Lat. by obs. 21.23s. Sailed by log 91 miles.

TUESDAY 1 JULY

Windy weather. At noon Cape Bon Esperance bore by acct. 641 leagues. Lat. by obs. 27.19. Sailed by log 102 miles.

WEDNESDAY 2 JULY

Hard squalls and showers with some lightning. Lat. by obs. 27.0 Sailed per log 84 miles.

FRIDAY 4 JULY

A large south easterly swell. At 3 pm found the fore top sail yard to be sprung. At 6 pm found the fore top mast stay broke. Cleaned between decks. Lat. by obs. 27.15 south. Sailed by log 42 miles.

FRIDAY 11 JULY

Unsettled weather, squally and very cold. A great number of Pintardo birds about the ship, with other birds called Albatrosses. A large south westerly swell. Lat. by obs. 33.10s. Sailed by log 111 miles.

SUNDAY 13 JULY

Great many of our men with violent colds and gripes, judging it to be owing to the change of the water, the Thames water being out. Lat. by obs. 33.14s. Sailed by log 46 miles.

---

[7] Presumably the island of that name in the Brazil Channel. 25s.30w.

Monday 14 July

Moderate weather, but cloudy with little wind and a large western swell. Very fine speckled birds about the ship (Course s67e Distance 60 miles Southing 33 miles Easting 55 miles). Lat. by obs. 33.50. Lat. by acct. 33.49 (miles distance 18.53e. Long. made 22.50e Difference of Long. 46e). Sailed by log 68 miles.

Wednesday 16 July

Moderate weather. Had a consultation of the ships' officers on the bridge: Quartermaster Bullard, Cooper mate, and Groves midshipman. The two former received 39 lashes by the Boatswain, the latter turned before the mast for stealing wine out of the hold, the property of Captain Skeddy r a.

Thursday 24 July

Cloudy. At 8 pm sounded no ground at 140 fathom. At 7 pm split the main top sail; at 7 am broke the starboard after futtock shrouds. At noon sounded no ground at 150 fathom. Lat. by obs. 35.38s. Sailed 78 miles.

Friday 25 July

Cloudy. s w swell, saw several gannets with a great number of other birds, the water much discoloured. At 4 pm broke a larboard futtock shroud. At noon brought to. Sounded ground at 127 fathom; firm gray sand mixed with ooze. Course s 7 e distance 61 miles southing 16 miles easting 59 miles. Difference of Long. 72e. Lat. by Obs. 35.17 Meridian distance 39.17e Long. Made of St Iago 49.3e. Sailed by log 68 miles.

Saturday 26 July

Light winds with pleasant weather and fine sky. At sunset saw the land n e b n, distance about 15 leagues. At 8 am sounded no ground at 150 fathom. At 11 am sounded no ground at 204 fathom. The bluff judged to lie between Cape Falso and Cape Lagullus, the departure taken from Cape Lagullus. Allowing it to bear by the compass n e b e distance about 18 leagues. Course with bearing included is n 24 w. Meridian distance 75 miles northing 68 westering 30° of longitude. Lat. by Obs. 35.33 south. Sailed by log 47 miles.

SUNDAY 27 JULY

Cloudy weather. A large irregular sea, with a strong southerly current. At 7 am discovered the foretop mast to be sprung in five places from 10 to 12 feet above the cap. Course s 8 7 e distance 31 miles southing 3 miles, easting 81 miles. Difference of Longitude 62E. Lat. by Obs. 36.17 Lat. by acct. 36.2s. Longitude made of Cape Lagullus 13.34. Sailed by log 57 miles.

THURSDAY 31 JULY

A fresh gale with hard squalls and a large sea from the westward. PM got the foretop mast, and a new top gallant mast at 6 pm. A squall lowered the mizzen yard.

FRIDAY 1 AUGUST

Fair weather with a large western swell. A M punished Truman Beamsley, seaman, with 39 lashes for stealing brandy out of the lazaretto. Many of the men troubled with colds and the scurvy.

SATURDAY 2 AUGUST

Unsettled weather. Got up top gallant yards. Opened the after hatches to get at copper, to bring the ship by the head. Found the ship to strain very much, and the main chains. The swell much abated since yesterday. Sailed by log 137 miles.

MONDAY 4 AUGUST

Pleasant weather. The caulker employed in caulking the long boat. Course N 6 9 E distance 70 miles northing 25 miles eastering 65 miles. Difference of Longitude made 78 east. Lat. by obs. 32.46. Lat. by acct. 32.48. Meridian distance 14.22E Long. of the Cape 16.27E. Sailed 80 miles.

TUESDAY 5 AUGUST

From St Iago. Stormy weather with hard squalls of wind, thunder, lightning and rain. The thunder very near us. The flashes of lightning very large and quick. About 3 am it entirely ceased, at which time had a pleasant breeze, smooth water, and a serene sky. A quarter of an hour before the squall there was a strong smell of sulphur, and after the squall was over a remarkable cloud to the northward, just above the horizon, appeared of many colours like sulphurous smoke. Split the main topsail and fore stay sail. Lat. by obs. 31.53s. Distance by log 81 miles.

SATURDAY 9 AUGUST
Dismal weather. By 7 am all the sails furled. Hauled main sail having nothing aboard but a triple reef in the fore sail. At 8 am the squall came on, with thunder, lightning and heavy rain; the sky all round very black. At 8.30 it broke away and we set sail. Sailed by log 46 miles.

SUNDAY 10 AUGUST
Bad weather. At 2 pm the clouds rising with hard squalls of thunder, lightning and very large hail and rain. Split the fore top sail. Reefed the sprit sail, handed main sail, main top sail and up fore sail. Nothing aboard but triple reef fore-top sail and fore stay sail which was split and the halyards of the stay sail broke. It came on in the most blackest, thickest clouds that any of the sailors ever saw. I am not able to express the dismal situation we were in, the hail and rain smashed the cabin windows, and poured in like a solid body, and passed in between decks clearing all before it. Though we received it but two points upon the quarter, it pulled the ship several streaks. It lasted about $1\frac{1}{2}$ minutes. Lat. by obs. 30.14 south. Sailed by log 64 miles.

MONDAY 11 AUGUST
Rainbow in the night. Unsettled weather. Flying squalls and rain; making preparation for putting into St Augustine's Bay in Madagascar. Course N 5 W. Distance 119 miles northing 118 miles difference of longitude 12 west. Lat. by obs. 28.8s. Lat. by account 28.6s. Meridian distance 17.45E. Longitude made of Cape Lagullus 20.25E. Distance by log 119 miles. Saw the rainbow one hour after it was dark; it appears very plain.

TUESDAY 12 AUGUST
Cloudy with small rains. Saw a shark, and many dolphins. (Some pintardo and pittards birds.) Tried with the jolly boat for a current and found one SEBE $3\frac{1}{2}$ fathom an hour. John Murphy, one of the company of soldiers, died. Committed his body to the deep. Prayers read by Captain Walpole. Lat. 26.58. Distance by log 66 miles.

WEDNESDAY 13 AUGUST
Towards Madagascar. Lowered down the jolly boat and scrubbed the ship's sides. Tried for a current but found none. Lat. by obs. 26.49. Sailed by log 6 miles.

MONDAY 18 AUGUST

Sight of Madagascar. Fresh gales with a large sea, pm. Saw land from the masthead. Bearing from SE to E at 5 degrees. Westminster Hall EBN. Berryhead EBS about 5 leagues at sunset; Berryhead and the southernmost part of land in sight off the nearest shore about 4 leagues. Saw a white patch of land which was taken to be Sandy Island bearing EBS about 5 miles. Stood off all night. At 8 am Westminster Hall ENE off shore about 5 leagues. At 10 am the extreme of the land NEBN to SBE. Sandy Island EBS about 3 miles. No ground at 45 fathom. Soon after the body of Sandy Island ESE about 2 miles. Found ground at 35 fathom – broken shells. The net cast 16 fathom the north breakers of Sandy Island EBN 2 miles: the least water 16 fathom bearing SEBE 1 mile. Standing in for the Bay with soundings from 16 to 11 fathom. At noon Westminster Hall NEBE.

TUESDAY 19 AUGUST

St Augustine's Bay. Light winds and variable. Soundings from 17 to 25, coarse sand then no ground at 166 fathom at 2 pm still had no ground at 5 pm. Berryhead ENE about $\frac{3}{4}$ mile. 11 fathom water. Next cast no ground. 20 fathom soon after. Tacked to the southward 21 fathom muddy ground. At 6 anchored in 10 fathom. Hoisted out the boats and at 6 am worked further in. At 9 am anchored in 13 fathom; Westminster Hall NE, Berryhead ENE. Tent rock SBE $\frac{3}{4}$ mile. Employed for watering; erected a tent for the ship's use. Found riding here the *Pelham, Edgecoat* and *Stretham*, which anchored in St Augustine's Bay one day before us. Received an ox from the *Edgecoat* which was very fine and tender – (or at least we all thought so.) Sailed from St Iago to Madagascar in 84 days.

WEDNESDAY 20 AUGUST

Madagascar. Light breezes from land and sea with fair weather. Received two boat loads of water which was very good, and one bullock. A report came to Major Chalmers from the *Stretham* of the death of Captain Farquharson who died of a flux on 29 July and was buried on 30. As soon as he was thrown over the Captain of the ship ordered 46 half-minute guns to be fired – it being his age. No news of the *Dodington*, we judging she is gone forward to an island called Johana. She was but poorly manned with sailors but we hope there is no danger, as she had 180 soldiers on board[8].

[8] She had in fact struck a rock and foundered.

1. 'The Old R.M.A. Woolwich in Wood's Time.' Paul Sandby.

2. *William Augustus, Duke of Cumberland, Captain General 1745–1757.*

3. *Lt. General James St Clair, Colonel 1st Foot 1737, Commander Land Forces L'Orient Expedition 1746.*

4. *'Some Artillery Equipments.'* From A Treatise on Artillery *by John Muller, Professor at R.M.A. 1741–1766.*

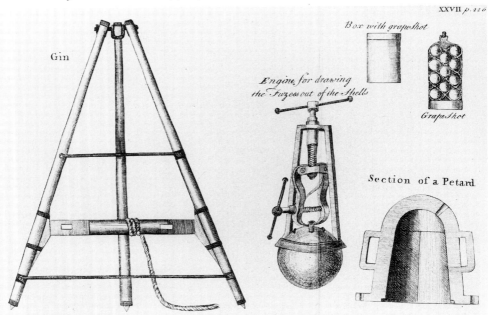

5. *Richard Lestock,* Admiral of the
Blue *1746, Commander Naval
Forces L'Orient. Died Dec. 1746.*

6. *David Hume, historian and
philosopher, Secretary to General St
Clair. By Carmintelle.*

7. *General Sir William Green 1725–
1811. Practitioner Engineer
L'Orient 1746. Chief Engineer
Great Siege Gibraltar 1779–1783.*

8. The Quay at L'Orient, showing French East Indiamen, 1776.

9. L'Orient and the Quiberon Peninsula. T. Jefferys' Maritime Parts of France.

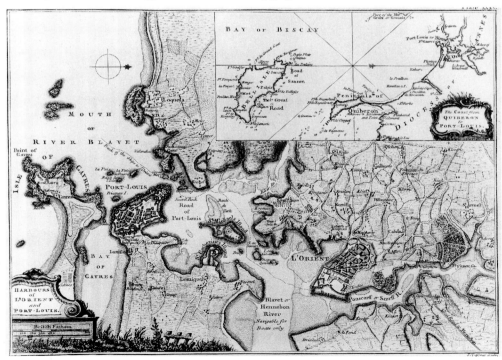

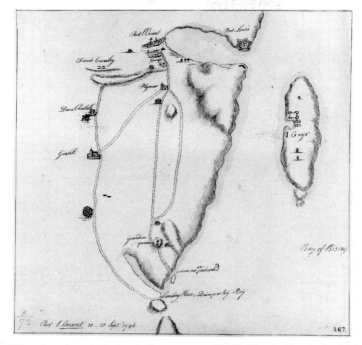

10. 'The Attack on L'Orient.' Contemporary Field Sketch. Cumberland Maps, Royal Library, Windsor.

11. 'An Artillery Night Shoot.' At L'Orient the furnace to heat the shot was left on board ship initially.

12. Gun and Mortar Batteries in action against a walled town.

13. A & B. British Land Service Brass Mortar. From a special handbook drawn in
the Ordnance Office for George, Prince of Wales, 1760.

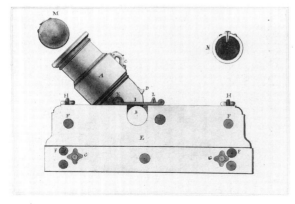

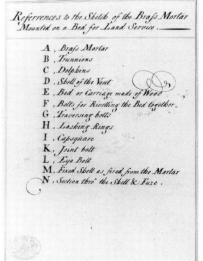

References to the Sketch of the Brass Mortar
Mounted on a Bed for Land Service.

A , *Brass Mortar*
B , *Trunnions*
C , *Dolphins*
D , *Shell of the Vent*
E , *Bed or Carriage made of Wood*
F , *Bolts for Rivetting the Bed together*
G , *Traversing bolts*
H , *Lashing Rings*
I , *Capsquare*
K , *Joint bolt*
L , *Eye Bolt*
M , *Fixed Shell as fired from the Mortar*
N , *Section thro' the Shell & Fuze.*

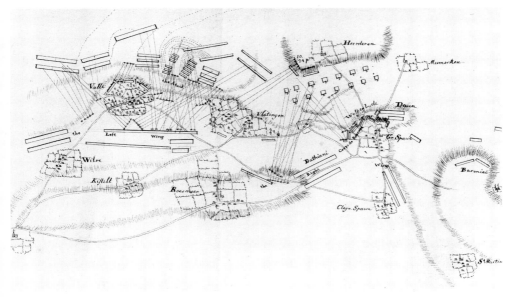

14. Plan of Battle of Val, with particular reference to artillery deployments, the British (Left Wing) being disposed in defence of Val. Arcs of both battalion and artillery train-guns are shown.

15. M.S. pages of Wood's diary describing 'The Battle of Maastricht Plain' generally known as Laufeld or Val.

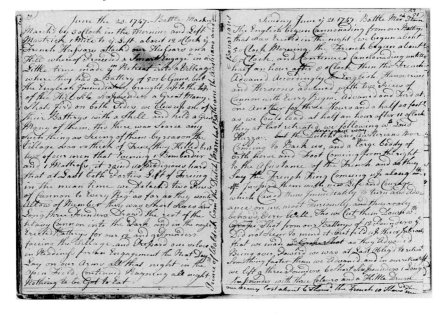

16. *The Great Highland Survey. A party escorted by the Royal Highland Regiment at Rannoch. Paul Sandby.*

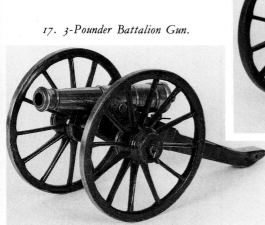

17. *3-Pounder Battalion Gun.*

18. *9-Pounder Field Gun with block trail.*

19. *A & B. The British brass field howitzer, as drawn for George, Prince of Wales, 1760.*

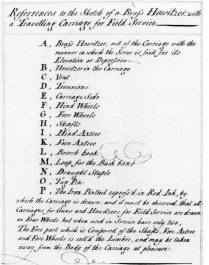

References to the Sketch of a Brass Howitzer, with a Travelling Carriage for Field Service

A, *Brass Howitzer, out of the Carriage with the manner in which the Screw is fixd for its Elevation or Depression*
B, *Howitzer in the Carriage*
C, *Vent*
D, *Trunnions*
E, *Carriage Side*
F, *Hind Wheels*
G, *Fore Wheels*
H, *Shafts*
I, *Hind Axtree*
K, *Fore Axtree*
L, *Breech hook*
M, *Loop, for the Back band*
N, *Draught Staple*
O, *Tug Pin*
P, *The Iron Pintail express'd in Red Ink, by which the Carriage is drawn, and it must be observed, that all Carriages, for Guns and Howitzers for Field Service are drawn on Four Wheels, but when used in Service have only two, The Fore part which is Composed of the Shafts, Fore Axtree and Fore Wheels is call'd the Limber, and may be taken away from the Body of the Carriage at pleasure.*

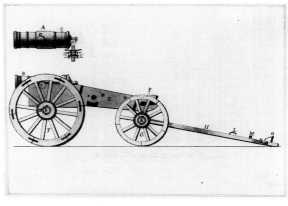

20. *A person in R.A. undress uniform engaged in Field Sketching. Possibly P. Sandby himself, by Francis Cotes.*

21. *Map of the Dee Valley by Braemar Castle by Lieutenant George Campbell from Wood's Company, R.A. that marched from Woolwich.*

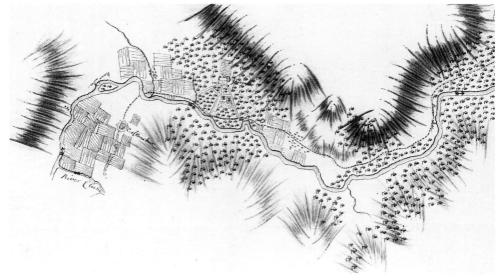

22. Jacobite prisoners under escort in the Highlands. Paul Sandby.

23. A view of the Tay Valley 1747. Paul Sandby.

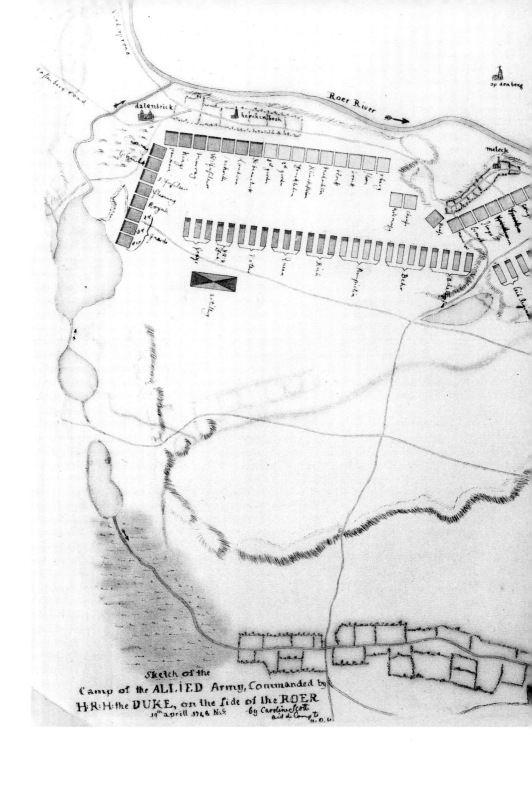

Sketch of the
Camp of the ALLIED Army, Commanded by
H.R.H. the DUKE, on the side of the ROER
19th aprill 1748 N.S.   by Caroline Scott
aid de Camp to
H.R.H.

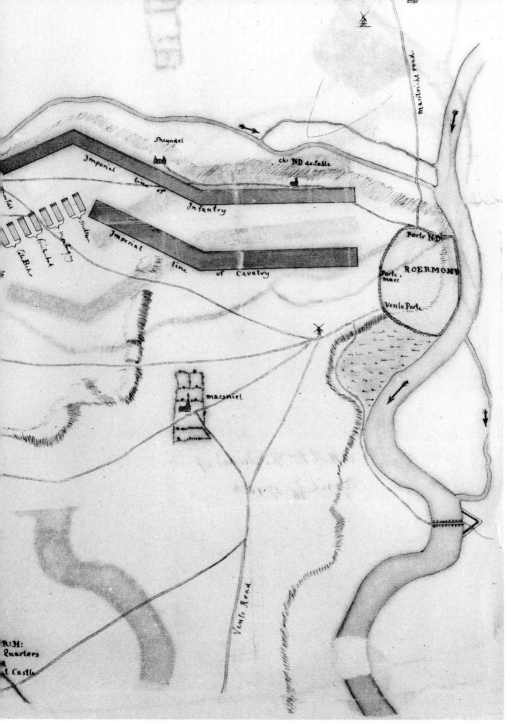

24. *Allied Camp near Roermond, April 1748. The Artillery Park is in front of the British Cavalry: The Greys and H.R.H.'s Dragoons. Drawn by Engineer A.D.C. Captain Caroline Scott, the defender of Fort William 1746. This is probably the location for the picture of the Royal Artillery by D. Morier on the dust cover.*

25. The Royal Highland Regiment practicing Fire and Movement on Glasgow Green 1757.

26. An East Indiaman. Such a ship embarked Wood's Company in 1755.

Com. in Ch. the Mafter Gen. Ordnance, Lᵗ Gˡ D. Marlborough.

Colonel en Second, the Lᵗ Gˡ Genˡ Sir J. Ligonier.

Colonel Commandant, William Belford, 8 Mar. 1751.	1	5	0
Lieutenant Colonel, Borgard Michelfen, ditto.	—	1	0
1 Major, George Williamfon ditto	—	0	15
2 Major, James Mace 1 Apr. 1756.	0	15	0
Major en Second, John Chalmers 1 Mar. 1755.	0	0	0

17 CAPTAINS 10 s.
Tho. Defauliers 1 Jan. 1745.
Thomas Flight   2 Oct.
Thomas Ord   1 Mar. 1746.
James Pattifon   1 Aug. 1747.
John Skeddy   1 Jan. 1748.
Alexander Leith 1 April 1749.
Charles Broome 8 Mar. 1751.
John Goodwin   1 Sept.
John Farquharfon 1 Mar. 1755.
Thomas James   ditto.
Richard Maitland   ditto.
Samuel Cleveland   ditto.
William Hyflop   ditto.
Robert Hind—
Ch. Farrington — } 29 Oct. 1755.
Jof. Brome —
Abr. Tovey — } 1 Apr. 1756.

Wm. Macleod
Alex. Campbell
ForbesMacbean } 1 Apr. 1756.
Fr. Ja. Buchanan

18 FIRST LIEUTS. 5 s.
CharlesStranover 1 April 1747.
Jacob Tovey   1 Mar. 1755.
Thomas Pike   - ditto.
Jofeph Winter - ditto.
Edw. Whitmore   ditto.
Griffith Williams   ditto.
John Macculloch
Geo. Charleton
SirCha.Chalmers
Jof. Barret —
Richard Edlin—
Thomas Huffey
David Hay
James Stephens
Will. Phillips
John York
And. Ferguffon
Geo. Anderfon } 1 Apr. 1756.

29 Oct. 1755.

19 CAPT. LIEUTENANTS 6 s.
Jacob Gregory   8 Mar. 1751.
John Northall   24 Mar. 1752.
Richard Mafon   ditto.
John Dovers   ditto.
Leonard Pattifon   ditto.
William Huffey   ditto.
Samuel Strechey   ditto.
William Martin   ditto.
Nathaniel Jones   ditto.
Borg. Michelfen
John Straton
John Jones   } 29 Oct. 1755.
Thomas Smith
Ph. Webdal
Peter Innes   29 Nov.

19 SECOND LIEUTS. 4 s.
David Rogers   1 Mar. 1755.
Horatio Spry   ditto.
Robert

Robert Hind
Benj. Stehelen
Dun. Drummond
Ja. Lawfon
Cha. Torriano } 29 Oc. 1755.
Tho. Howdell
James Butler
David Mukel
Geo. Forman   29 Nov.
John Molman
Tho. Baker
Geo. Lewis
David Day
Tho. Blomer } 1 Ap. 1756.
John Carter
Jof. Walton.
Tho. Sheperd

Jofiah Jeffrys   ditto.
John Smith   ditto.
William Corbet   ditto.
Daniel Sweet   ditto.
Alexand. Johnfon   ditto.
John Scott   ditto.
John M'Culloch   ditto.
Samuel Glegg   24 Apr. 1755.
David Delacour,   1 July 1755.
Edward James
Barth. Belford
Geo. Phœnix
Chrift. Schalk
Anth. Farrington
Henry Skinner
John Michelfen
Edw. Morgan } 29 Oc. 1755.
John Pomroy
John Williamfon
John Wilfon
Peter Trail
Ellis Walker
David Standifh
John Bradbridge
Thomas Jones
William Johnfon } 29 Nov.

55 LT. FIRE-WORKERS, 3 s. 8 d.
James Halfall   13 Jan. 1753.
Prim. Elphinftone 1 Mar. 1755.
William Gofling   ditto.
Jonathan Lewis   ditto.
George Campbell   ditto.
Thomas Rogers   ditto.
Alexan. Chalmers   ditto.
Robert Hetzler   ditto.
Thomas Collins   ditto.
George Groves   ditto.
William Bowen   ditto.
Edward Foy   ditto.
William Venner   ditto.
Flemming Martin   ditto.
John Chalmers   ditto.

Tho. Simpfon
Thomas Davis
Jof. Eyre
William Hill
Peter Martin
Wm. Borthwick
William Gray
Sam. Harrifon } 1 Ap. 1756.
Nath. Conner
Agar Wightman
James Donnellan
Wm. Harris
Geo. Skipton
John Carden

Chaplain, Montagu Parfon, ——	0	6	8
Adjutant, Capt. Lt. Forbes Macbean, 1 Apr. 1756.	0	5	0
Quarter Mafter, William Phillips, 1 Apr. 1750.	0	6	0
Bridge Mafter, Nathaniel Marfh,	0	5	0
Surgeon, James Irwin, —— 15 Dec. 1749.	0	4	0
Mate, William Hobfon, 1 Mar. 1755.	0	2	6

Agent, James Cockburn, King ftreet, Golden Square
Expls &

27. *The Army List 1756. The first entry recording the Royal Regiment of Artillery. James Wood was still a cadet at this time, but many of those named appear in his Diary.*

28. *Captain John Skeddy, R.A., who took a Company to Bombay in 1755. He died at Surat, 1759.*

29. *Vice-Admiral Sir Charles Watson. Commanded the R.N. Squadron in Indian Waters 1755–1757.*

30. *Sir William James, Bart. Commodore of the East India Company's Bombay Marine. Serving 1747–59 in the East.*

31. False Bay, Cape of Good Hope.

32. The Green, Bombay.

33. The Bombay Grab, *1776. An armed ketch of the Bombay Marine.*

34. The attack with fireships on Fort Geriah, 1756, after P. Canot.

35. Bombay Fort, with shipping off.

36. View of Surat, showing the European factories.

37. *Lt. Colonel Robert Clive with Mir Jaffir after Plassey.*

38. *The Peshwa of the Mahratta Empire.*

39. *A scene outside Pondicherry.*

40. *The ruins of Pondicherry by Engineer John McClean who is seated left foreground.*

41. *A 24-pounder heavy brass gun with field carriage.*

42. *A siege battery showing both Royal Artillery and British Infantry, 1762. The scene is at Havana by D. Serres.*

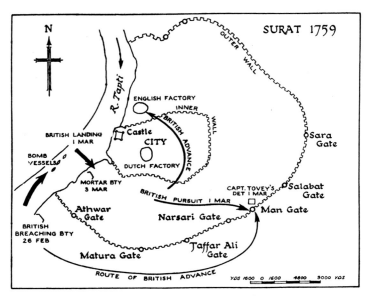

43. Reproduced from the Royal Artillery Journal, 1951.

44. Map of Operations, Pondicherry, 1760–61. Cumberland Maps, Royal Library, Windsor.

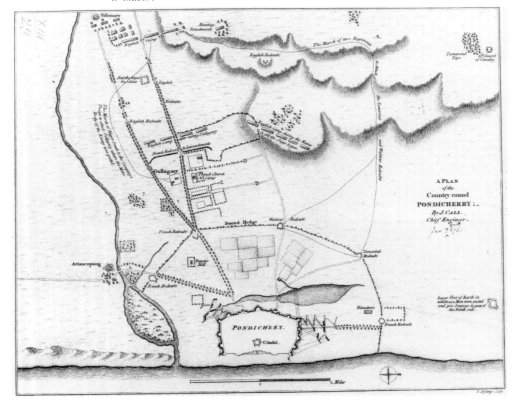

The inhabitants of this island are black and are either pagans or Mahometans; though a savage kind of people yet they seem to have a good deal of natural morality and are very civil to the English. They go mostly naked with nothing but a bandage round their middle and a cloth between their legs and tucked in, behind and before, to the bandage. Their grander sort wear a woollen cloth or wrapper over one shoulder, Highland fashion; their wrappers are generally worked round with beads, large and small, which they are very fond of, as likewise buttons, knives, needles, scissors, buckles, rings and all sort of toys and handkerchiefs, especially firelocks, flints and gunpowder. They have for their arms javelins, lances, bows and arrows which they are very dextrous with and really can shoot with the firelock very well. They have a sort of leaves which being chewed exhilarates, and if taken too much makes them mad for 2 or 3 days. The most pernicious animals are crocodiles and great serpents, though I do not hear of any harm they do. The women are discreet and virtuous though the poorer sort common enough and are very fond of ribbons and garters. They are governed by several Kings, and are continually at war, one with the other, about their cattle and slaves; yet unanimous enough to defend themselves against the invasion of strangers. Almost every province has its peculiar dialect, but not so different that they understand one another. The air of this island is very wholesome and the soil very fruitful in many parts affording everything necessary for the life of Man. There are very fine oxen, sheep, goats, fowls, lemons, calabashes etc. with plenty of rice, hides, wax, gum, crystals, ebony and wood of all sorts, with pleasant valleys and fine rivers. Their priests are reckoned wizards and live in hordes [sic] under a Chief.; money does not pass but they will barter with us for guns and powder, knives and toys – they will give a bullock for about 6 or 8 pounds of powder, the same for an old firelock, and sheep, lambs, goats, and fowls for balls and flints. These bullocks are really very fat and good, maybe worth about £9 or £10 in England. They have a dexterous way of catching them by slinging a rope with a noose over their head and forefoot and then drawing them to a tree. This island lies in about 26 to 12 South Latitude, and runs about from s w to n e and in Longitude from London 48 to 50 East and is one of the largest islands in the world, producing plenty of fish.

Thursday 21 August

Madagascar. Taking in fresh water and provisions. Another party of the sailors on shore salting the meat in the tent. Sent the Artillery soldiers on shore with a number of tents for them.

Friday 22 August

Pleasant weather. The artillery on shore learning their exercise, the sick beginning to recover their healths.

Saturday 23 August

Madagascar. Sent the carpenter on shore to cut wood for the ships' use. The large swell and spring tides have prevented the long boat from watering, it being brackish. One of the E I Company's men had his arm broke in two or three places helping to get in water. Major Chalmers and Commissary Walker muster the three companies on board and shore, when Captain/Lieutenant Northall was made Captain in the room of Captain Farquharson, deceased, from the 20 instant; Jacob Tovey made Captain/Lieutenant, Sir Charles Chalmers First Lieutenant and Campbell second lieutenant and Cadet Wood Lieutenant Fireworker[9].

Sunday 24 August

Getting wood and water, and salting the beef on shore, a great scarcity of salt, very little about the Island.

Monday 25 August

Lieutenant Fireworker James Wood was ordered on board the *Edgecoat*, Captain Pierce, in the room of Captain Northall, who was ordered on board the *Stretham* to take charge of his Company in the room of Captain Farquharson deceased.

Tuesday 26 August

Pleasant weather. The artillery learning the small gun exercise. The drummers and fifers practising; the sick belonging to the artillery on shore much better but several of the sailors still troubled with scurvy.

Wednesday 27 August

Madagascar. Pleasant weather. Getting on board water, bullocks, fowls, mutton etc; the black people busy in bringing bullocks etc.

Thursday 28 August

Weather as yesterday. Orders to strike the artillery tents, and to be received on board with the people all pretty well recovered. It's very remarkable that there is a land breeze in the morning and a sea breeze

---

[9] The author promoted to the lowest officer rank – below a second lieutenant.

in the afternoon and yet there is a fresh water river that meets the sea. Notwithstanding, they are so near you may have salt water at one side of the boat and fresh at the other side.

Friday 29 August
Pleasant weather. Getting the rest of the artillery on board, as likewise several bullocks, cows, goats etc, fowls and vegetables. Unmoored at 8 pm and waited for the Commodore's motion.

Saturday 30 August
At 7 am weighed with a light breeze s e. Steered at w n w to n w. Had no ground at 30 fathom. The northmost land in sight n e b n distance offshore 5 or 6 leagues, the other ships astern, under sail; all in good health.

Remained 11 days at Madagascar.

Sunday 31 August
Left Madagascar. Sailed with a fine pleasant gale in company with the *Pelham, Stretham* and *Houghton*. Sounded in the night, had no ground at 40 fathom. At noon the extreme of the land in sight bore s e b s to e b s. Distance about 9 leagues: the departure taken from Westminster Hall allowing it to lie in the latitude 23.27s and longitude from London 44.26e with bearing e s e. Sailed by log 79 miles.

Wednesday 3 September
Pleasant weather. At 10 am saw the island of St Christopher n e b n. Distance 5 leagues. It is a low shrubby land. At the north end there is a large sandy beach and a bluff point. At noon it bore n b e. Distance 3 leagues. Lat. by Obs. 17.12s. Sailed 88 miles.

Thursday 4 September
Kept the lead going in the night. Had no ground at 60 fathom; in the morning Richard Jones, one of the company's soldiers, died and was buried in the evening. At 6 pm the island bore s e b e 5 or 6 leagues. The departure taken in Lat. 17.6s. Lat. by Obs. 16.29s. Sailed by the log 55 miles.

Monday 8 September
Weather and company as before. Sounded in the night: had no ground 70 fathom. Saw the island of Comoro, bearing n e b e Distance 10 or 12 leagues. Course n 1 1 e Distance 50 miles. Difference of Lat. 50 departure 9. Difference of Long. 10. Lat. by obs. 12.5s. Meridian

distance of Christopher 16 west Longitude of London 43.23E. Sailed by log 52 miles.

TUESDAY 9 SEPTEMBER
Kept a good look out in the night and sounded at 5 am: the body of Comoro bore EBN distance 12 leagues at 8 degrees bore east, distance 12 or 13 leagues Lat. by obs. 11.53S. Sailed 48 miles.

WEDNESDAY 10 SEPTEMBER
Pleasant weather. Company as before. Smooth water and at 8 am tried the current and found it set SEBE, 3 fathom per hour. Lat. by obs. 11.40. Sailed by log 20 miles.

THURSDAY 11 SEPTEMBER
From Madagascar. Cloudy rainy weather am. Caught two sharks each between 8 and 9 feet long. One of them had 12 young ones in its belly, the least of which was 20 inches long. Also struck a pilot fish of about 12 inches long. At 5 pm the body of Comoro[10] bore ESE distance about 15 leagues. The departure taken from there allowing it to lie in the Lat. 11.50s and Long. from London 43.50E. Course with bearings and distance N80W. Distance 48 miles, X of Latitude 9 Departure 48; difference of Long. 49. Lat. by obs. 11.42. Lat. by Acc. 11.41. Meridian distance off Comoro 00.48W. Longitude of London 43.00E. Sailed by the log 17 miles.

SUNDAY 21 SEPTEMBER
Weather as before – fair. PM our consorts a great way ahead. Hoisted their colours and crowded all their sail. Course N46E. Lat. by obs. 0.59S. Sailed by log 104 miles.

MONDAY 22 SEPTEMBER
Pleasant breeze. Saw our consorts right ahead at a great distance. Lat. observed 0.10N. Crossed the line the second time. Course N36E. Sailed by log 76 miles.

WEDNESDAY 24 SEPTEMBER
Fair weather. At 5 am saw the land at NNE to NNW. Distance 4 or 5 leagues. Sounded no ground at 35 fathom. At 8 am saw it from NWBN to NNE. Distance of the nearest point 5 or 6 leagues. At noon the extreme of the land from the masthead at NE to NNW. Can see the

---

[10] Comoro Islands lie at the northern exit of the Mozambique Channel.

Houghton's hull; the other two ships just in sight under the land. This land is called the Madagascar shore: Lat. by obs. 2.54N. Sailed by log 99 miles.

THURSDAY 25 SEPTEMBER
Fair weather. In company with *Houghton*. The *Pelham* and *Stretham* left us. Took our departure from the land of Vello on the Madagascar shore as it bore yesterday. Lat. 3.26N. Sailed by log 136 miles.

FRIDAY 26 SEPTEMBER
From Madagascar. Cloudy weather. A great many birds called Boobys about the ship. Course N 8 2 E. Lat. by obs. 3.53 and acct. 3.42N. Sailed by log 118 miles in company with the *Houghton*.

SATURDAY 18 OCTOBER
In company with the *Houghton*. From Monday 6th to this day nothing material only drove backwards and forwards with strong currents. Made but two degrees to the northward in these 12 days. We imagine ourselves to be near shore by the quantity of different kind of birds, some of which we caught. A great number of sharks about the ship one of which we caught measured 10′2″ with several rows of teeth. Sounded no ground at 50 fathom. Course N 1 8 E. Lat. by obs. 11.30N. Sailed by log those 12 days 554 miles.

SUNDAY 19 OCTOBER
Sultry hot. At 6 am saw the land from N to NWBN. Distance 12 or 14 leagues which is imagined to be the Island of Socotra, having reason to expect we should see it – by our variation increasing, though by our accounts we are two hundred leagues to the eastward of it. At noon the extreme of the land from NBW to NNW. Distance 14 or 16 leagues. Course until noon NE. Meridian distance from Vello on the Madagascar shore 10.22E. Variation 8.52W. Lat. by obs. 12.0 N. Sailed by log 15 miles.

TUESDAY 21 OCTOBER
In company with the *Houghton*. Fair weather. At sunrise, a bluff cheek on Socotra bore NBWBW and the westernmost land NW. Distance 12 leagues. This island is high land and very remarkable as seen in the draught I took at noon: the body of the island bore NWBW distance 16 leagues[11]. Sailed by log 16 miles.

[11] Wood evidently was trained to make drawings. None have survived.

FRIDAY 24 OCTOBER

From Madagascar. Light winds and fair as for several days past. A great number of dolphins, pilot fish, skip jacks etc. with several kinds of birds about the ship. Course N 8 0 E. Lat. by obs. 11.0N. Sailed by log 42 miles.

SATURDAY 25 OCTOBER

Fair weather. In the night lost sight of the *Houghton,* we imagined she did not tack when we tacked though we made the usual signal. Course N86E. Lat. by obs. 10.43. Sailed 51 miles, strong southerly current.

SUNDAY 26 OCTOBER

Fair weather. At 8 am saw the *Houghton* to the leeward and bore down to her. Caught some dolphins which is a very fine straight fish with divers colours when alive, but when dead the colours fade away. Several little hog fish about the rudder following the ship. Current still continues. Lat. by obs. 10.3N. Sailed by log 38 miles.

SATURDAY 15 NOVEMBER

Nothing material happening from 27 October to this day. Drove about with strong southerly currents; made but 6 degrees to the northward but different kinds of birds about the ship a few days ago, with several sorts of fish, and last Monday hoisted our colours, being His Majesty's birthday. At 1 pm fired 21 guns, and the artillery three rounds with their small arms and at night had an illumination with several candles burning in the shrouds; and on Tuesday 4th inst lay to for the *Houghton,* who sprung her foretop mast. Sent our carpenter to assist in putting up another; the sailors employed in clearing between decks and taking down the cabins; making all ready in case of meeting with Angria[12], the pirate, as we imagine we shall sail near his principal port called Gheria; the sailors practising the long gun exercise, and several of the sailors have learned the small gun exercise by seeing our people exercise every day. Our men begin to fall down with the scurvy, sultry hot and short allowance of water. Course E B S Distance 78 miles. Difference of Lat. 15. Departure 17. Meridian distance at Socotra

---

[12] Angria was a Mahratta private soldier who led a revolt in the Deccan and then took to organized piracy against European trade along the Malayan coast. He successfully corrupted his nominal rulers by gifts of booty, so gaining a free hand at sea, and maintaining a force of armed galleys. His main base was south of Bombay.

10.9E. Variation by meridian 5. Azimuth 5 w. Sailed those 19 days by log 1101 miles.

SUNDAY 16 NOVEMBER
In company with the *Houghton*. At 2 am Will Bromfield, Gunner, RA, died. Committed his body to the waves. Lat. observed 15.53. Course s and E. Sailed by log 87 miles.

MONDAY 17 NOVEMBER
Saw some dolphins and several flying fish about 10 or 12 inches long who can fly while their wings are wet. Lat. of 15.35N. Sailed 31 miles from Madagascar.

TUESDAY 18 NOVEMBER
Fair weather sounded in the night. Had no ground at 80 fathoms. Saw a hawk fly about the ship. Lat. 15.27N. Sailed by log 76 miles.

WEDNESDAY 19 NOVEMBER
A great number of our soldiers bad with the scurvy. Lat. 15.24N. Sailed by log 63 miles.

THURSDAY 20 NOVEMBER
In company with the *Houghton*. Squalls and small rains. Saw a hawk and some very remarkable fish of a flat kind with a horn on their backs and a very small mouth. They are about 10 inches long. They are of beautiful colours, but lose it when taken out of the water. Lat. 15.28N. Sailed 51 miles.

FRIDAY 21 NOVEMBER
Above $\frac{1}{4}$ of our company down with the scurvy. Sounded in the night, but had no ground at 120 fathoms. Lat. 16.6N. Sailed by log 32 miles.

SUNDAY 23 NOVEMBER
Sultry hot. At 6 pm tried the current and found it set NWBN at 5 fathom. Sounded in the night but had no ground at 120 fathoms. Saw a great number of dolphins and some small sharks. Course N 5 0 E. Distance 10 miles. Difference of latitude, departure 6 miles distance of Socotra. 17.39E. Lat. obsn 16.24 and by Acct. 16.14 north. Sailed by log 9 miles.

MONDAY 24 NOVEMBER

Sounded in the night. Had no ground at 75 fathom. At daylight saw
2 sail to the windward which we take to be trading gallivats[13], being
but very small. Our men increasing every day with the scurvy and 3
or 4 with the fever. Lat. by obs. 16.31N. Sailed by log 20 miles.

WEDNESDAY 26 NOVEMBER

Fine weather. At 6 am we struck ground with the lead at 50 fathoms:
ooze and sand. Saw a great many snakes and abundance of weeds. At
10 am saw the land from E to NE, distance 10 or 11 leagues. Course
ENE. Lat. by obs 17.11N. Sailed by log 74 miles.

THURSDAY 27 NOVEMBER

Pleasant weather. Sounded: found ground from 35 to 20 fathom. The
land in sight about 6 leagues. At sunset the extreme of the land in
sight. Near 1/3 of our company down with the scurvy. John Emerson,
mattross died at 11.30 of a fever and flux. Lat. by obs. 17.36N. Sailed
50 miles.

FRIDAY 28 NOVEMBER

Fair weather. At 6 pm the extreme of the land bore NEBN to ESE.
Distance 9 leagues. At noon the extreme of the land from EBS to NE,
distance 8 or 10 leagues. Committed the dead body to the sea; our men
with the scurvy much better, as we imagine its owing to the smell that
comes off land. Lat. by obs. 18.6 variation for meridian 1°23W. Sailed
42 miles.

SATURDAY 29 NOVEMBER

Weather as yesterday. In the company of the *Houghton*. Stood in until
12 o'clock into 17 fathoms. At daylight saw a sail to the north standing
towards us. At 10 am she hoisted a broad red pendant and fired a gun
to the leeward under Red Colours. At noon her boat came on board,
and informed us she was the company's ship called the *Protector*,
commanded by Commodore James[14]. Saluted him with 11 guns; he
returned the same number. At noon the extreme of the land bore from
NNEBE to SSBE, distance 8 leagues. Lat. by obs. 18.36N.

---

[13] Oared galleys with sails. Used by Angria as armed galleys against commerce.

[14] C-in-C of the Bombay Marine. A monument to his memory crowns Shooters
Hill, Woolwich. See D.N.B. entry.

SUNDAY 30 NOVEMBER

St Andrew's Day. Pleasant weather. Stood in with a sea breeze until 10 pm when the commodore made the signal to anchor which we did in 8 fathoms. Soft ground. At 7 am weighed, the wind at NEBE. Saw the Flag and Staff of Bombay, bore NEBE. Malabar Hill bore NNEBE and Savage Castle E. Distance off the nearest shore 2 leagues. At 9 came to an anchor in 9 fathoms, soft mud. The ships in harbour NEBN; Malabar Hill NBEBE.

Bombay at a distance of 7 or 8 leagues: held regular soundings from 9 to 8 fathoms. At 2 past Meridian weighed and stood in; had soundings from 8 to 4 fathoms. Saluted the flag in Bombay harbour with 15 guns and came to an anchor a little after. The Red flag was on board the HMS *Kent* Admiral Watson, 70 guns; found also riding here the HMS *Cumberland*, Admiral Pocock, 64 guns; HMS *Tiger* 60 guns, Captain Latham; HMS *Salisbury* 50 guns, Captain Knowles: HMS *Bridgewater*, 20 guns, Captain Martin, and the *Kingfisher* sloop, Captain Smith, with 4 of the company's bomb ketches, viz: the *Drake, Viper, Warren* and the *Triumph* prawn with several gallivats, armed vessels and trading ships, all in the company's service. Found also riding here the *Pelham* EIM, Captain Lindsey, the *Stretham*, Captain Mason. They both anchored here on 5 and 6 November, as likewise the *Dragon* EIM who left England six weeks after us; notwithstanding, she anchored here six weeks before us. No news of the *Dodington* EIM, Captain Sampson, as yet. We imagine she has sailed for Madras to land the company of artillery[15]. Saluted the fort with fifteen guns who returned the same number. 93 days passage from Madagascar to Bombay, 84 days from St Iago to Madagascar, and 29 days from the Downs to St Iago, being all the sailing days from the Downs 206 days, or 29 weeks and 3 days; but from our embarkation at Gravesend to our disembarking at Bombay 254 days, or 36 weeks and 2 days. Sailed by log from the downs to St Iago 2666; from St Iago to Madagascar by log 7437, and from Madagascar to Bombay 5643. In all from the Downs to Bombay 15,746 miles.

---

[15] It is true she was carrying the Royal Artillery Company for Madras, but she had struck a rock in Algoa Bay and lost all but 23 passengers and crew. The rock on Bird Island is now marked by the Dodington Light, near Port Elizabeth. Three R.A. survivors reached India after extraordinary adventures.

SERVICE IN INDIA
NOVEMBER 1755 – MAY 1760

Short description of Bombay Latt 19 Long W72.20

In the Mogul Empire an island in Asia formerly belonged to the King of Portugal who transferred it in the year 1663 to King Charles II as part of the Infanta Catherine's portion upon her marriage with him who afterwards made a present of it to the English East India Company. The island is about $7\frac{1}{2}$ miles in length and between 3 and 4 in breadth which is inhabited by English, Portuguese and people of different nations as Mohammets, Pagoons[1] etc. The island is very rocky and produces rice, cocoa trees etc. and lies convenient for trade. The harbour is able to contain 600 sail of ships. The town is near a mile in length, the number of people on the island is computed to be between seven or eight hundred thousand[2]. The place is reckoned now very healthful, though excessively hot in the months of March, April, May and June, but the SW monsoon coming in about the middle of June cools the air with frequent showers of rain which last until near the latter end of August. There is a tolerable good fort, and good fortifications round the town, with a wet ditch and several forts on the island, Viz: Mazagon, Dungaree, Syon, Riva, Alorlee, Mayam and Surree. The island is about 19 or 20 miles in circumference. All on the island are allowed a free exercise of their religion. There is a fort on Butcher's Island about 5 miles from the island Bombay which is an officers command. There is another island called the Allophanto (opposite to Butcher's Island) which place is cut out of the rocks with figures of men and women, about fourteen foot high, all in rows, and cut out of the solid rock. There are several subterranean passages the end of which is not known, but they are mostly full of water, wherein if you discharge a musket you have an echo for about a minute and an innumerable number of

---

[1] A word commonly used to describe Hindus.

[2] This is a gross exaggeration – somewhere about 100,000 probably.

[94]

large bats flying out on the echo. There are several lofty passages with a great number of pillars all cut out of the rock.

Their marriages in Bombay of some of their castes of religion are very singular. In the forenoon they send a long train of women with presents from the bridegroom to the bride marching with tom toms (a sort of drum) before them; there is an empty palankeen carried in the rear for the use of the bride from her house to her husband's, and at night the bride and bridegroom are carried in state through the town with lights and music before them, and at the end of every street fireworks are let off. They have also dancing girls in their train, who have a very odd and ridiculous dance. The parents of the married couple send presents to their friends. The married couple have no choice, as they are generally married before they are capable either to choose or refuse, being often married at 5 or 6 years of age, but do not cohabit before the bride is twelve and the bridegroom something older. As to their burials the Gentoo[3] burn their dead, and the greatest honour the Parsees think they can do to the remains of their dearest friends is to expose the corpse to be devoured by birds of prey, looking upon these living sepulchres to be preferable to any other sort of tomb. Accordingly they have a place at Malabar Hill about two miles from Bombay, surrounded with a wall about ten foot high and about 23 foot wide, the ground within being raised six foot with a slope to the centre, that the moisture may drain from the carcasses into a sink in the middle of the building. Nothing can be more shocking than a view of their dead bodies, loathsome and discoloured, some yellow, others green, some with their eyes torn out, some with their flesh torn off their cheeks, holes eaten in several parts of their bodies and their flesh torn off their bones. Some of their skins are hardened by the sun like tanned leather and others clean picked by the vultures etc. When the bones are quite rotten they sweep them into the sink to make room for other bodies. It would be tedious to mention the many absurdities they have amongst their different sects of religion. The first caste never eats anything but what dies naturally; that is they kill nothing; others again never cut or comb their hair and besmear their bodies and faces with ashes. Some of their Brahmins (Gentoo Priests) sit at their pagodas (their place of worship) all day long throwing ashes every now and then over their bodies; one in particular sitting quite naked under the shade of a tree with a hole bored through the skin of his privy member with a large ring fixed in the hole. This fellow was much revered by the married women who prostrate themselves before him, and take hold of the

[3] Hindus.

member devoutly in their hand and kiss it, while the owner strokes their heads muttering some prayer for their prolification etc. There are other Brahmins who have a large hole made in the ground with a cover over it, where they remain ten or twelve days living on nothing but a few grains of rice a day and some water. These are put in at a small hole in the cover by those who attend them. If they survive this and perform it thirty times they are assured they merit heaven. I saw one of these men taken out at Byculla and he really looked more like a corpse than a living man.

Monday 1 December 1755
This morning Major Chalmers, Captain Skeddy and Maitland went on shore, and in the evening Skeddy's and Maitland's companies disembarked and took their quarters in the barracks on Bombay Green. Captain Northall's company being landed about three weeks before, he had prepared quarters etc. against the arrival of the above two companies.

Tuesday 2 December
The officers of the two companies were presented by Major Chalmers to Colonel Clive where they dined and supped. Orders by Major Chalmers for our men to be out every morning on the green to learn their exercise, and all those men to send in their names to their captains which worked in the Laboratory at Woolwich. We are sending all our sick into the hospital, some of whom are very bad with the scurvy and flux.

Thursday 4 December
The officers belonging to the two companies presented by Colonel Clive to Governor Bourchier. Orders for a muster by Major Chalmers tomorrow morning.

Friday 5 December
The three companies mustered. We are having to send a great many of our men every day to the hospital occasioned by their drinking new arrack. Two paroles to be given out every day: the one a military parole and the other a militia parole.

Saturday 6 December
A court martial held on Patrick Low, mattross, for being absent from muster for which he was picquetted. Orders that a lieutenant of each company attends the parade at gun firing in the morning and in the

afternoon at 4 pm, in order to see the men go through their exercise and to attend constantly. Men to parade for church tomorrow at 10 am.

SUNDAY 7 DECEMBER
Military Parole [password] Cambridge and Militia Parole Canton – Captain Northall's company to be ready with four officers to march to the gun and mortar exercise on Tuesday, the Captain to appoint the officers. Captain Maitland and Lieutenant Sir Charles Chalmers for the day.

MONDAY 8 DECEMBER
Paroles as a company of H M Artillery is to march to Byculla tomorrow. This evening the barrack master is to furnish them with provisions, drams and other allowances of that nature usually given to the party of artillery there. Captain Northall and Lieutenant Scott for the day.

TUESDAY 8 DECEMBER
Captain Northall's company march from hence to Byculla to practice with the guns and mortars. 82 men sick in the hospital. Exercise as usual.

TUESDAY 16 DECEMBER
Last night about 9 pm one of the inhabitants killed by some of the men of war's men. Hugh Collins, mattross, punished by the sentence of a court martial.

FRIDAY 19 DECEMBER
Marched from here a party of the R A to relieve Captain Northall's company in order to carry on the practice of the guns and mortars at Byculla.

THURSDAY 1 JANUARY 1756
Muster of the three companies of the R A and a company sent to Byculla to relieve the other.

THURSDAY 8 JANUARY
The company of the R A at Byculla was relieved by a detachment of the company's artillery and the practice to be carried on by them.

WEDNESDAY 14 JANUARY
Received our arrears for the year 1755 to 1 January 1756.

SUNDAY 25 JANUARY
Received the Batta[4] allowed by the Honourable EI Company for
quarters etc. from 30 November 1755 to this day, which was to each
Captain and Captain/Lieutenant for a month of 31 days 100 rupees,
each lieutenant $34\frac{1}{2}$. Major Chalmers made Lieutenant Winter a
Captain/Lieutenant, Lieutenant Barrett First Lieutenant, Lieutenant
Lewis Second Lieutenant and Mr Vans, Surgeon, Lieutenant
Fireworker in the room of Captain/Lieutenant Strachey who did not
come to India on this command. Barrett was made up in England 29
October 1755.

TUESDAY 27 JANUARY
Marched from here this morning three companies of the RA, two
companies of artillery and one company of infantry to encamp at
Byculla.

WEDNESDAY 28 JANUARY
A company of infantry embarked on Board EIM *Edgecoat* bound for
Surat and Macao.

SATURDAY 31 JANUARY
The King's and Company's artillery with one company of infantry
were reviewed by Governor Bourchier, the two Admirals, Watson
and Pocock, and Colonel Clive. After the review all the officers
breakfasted with the Governor and Admirals in camp. The same
morning EIM *Pelham* (Captain Lindsey) sailed for England. This
afternoon it was in orders for the detachment of the RA to hold
themselves in readiness to embark at an hour's warning.

TUESDAY 3 FEBRUARY
This morning the King's and Company's artillery marched from
Byculla and came to their quarters at Bombay.

---

[4] Batta. An extra cash allowance paid voluntarily by the E.I. Company. The
King's Army was paid by the Crown, but E.I. Company were to provide
quarters, bedding, heat and light.

FRIDAY 6 FEBRUARY

Gheria. This morning embarked the three companies of the RA with two companies of the Company's artillery commanded by Captain Carter and Captain Galleard and a detachment of Swiss infantry, commanded by Captains Govin and Ziegler[5]. Captain Skeddy's and Captain Galleard's company on board HMS *Kent*, Captain Maitland's and a detachment of infantry on board HMS *Cumberland*, Captain Northall's and the remainder of the Swiss on board HMS *Salisbury* and Captain Carter's company on board HMS *Tiger*, Colonel Clive and Major Chalmers on board the *Kent*. A signal from the *Kent* for unmooring and we were ready for sailing the next morning.

SATURDAY 7 FEBRUARY

Towards Gheria. At 7 am a signal for sailing. At 8 all were under weigh in company with 3 bomb ketches, store ships, gallivats and several small craft for landing troops at Gheria which was the place we are going to attack. Sailed by Bombay Fort with a pleasant land breeze. The fort saluted Admiral Pocock with 15 guns which was returned with the same number.

SUNDAY 8 FEBRUARY

These 24 hours pleasant weather. Sailed by Old Woman island, 2 miles offshore. Saw two sail to the SW. At 9.30 am the *Bombay* grab[6] and *Drake* ketch joined our fleet. The *Content* sloop and three gallivats joined at 11 am. Ghoul island ENE, the extreme of Rajapore SEBE distance off shore 4 or 5 leagues.

MONDAY 9 FEBRUARY

At 1.30 am saw 7 sail of gallivats to the southward belonging to Angria. At sunset the southernmost land in sight: offshore 6 or 7 miles, pleasant weather.

---

[5] A Swiss company entered the company's service in Bombay in 1752 under Alexander de Ziegler. They were not kept together as a unit and there was considerable desertion.

[6] An E.I. Marine locally constructed gunboat, based on a two-masted Arab coasting vessel.

Tuesday 10 February

At sunrise Cape Dobs s s e and Ziga (Jaigadh): Fore bore n e b e: distance offshore 3 or 4 miles. At noon Anti Gheria s e b s, distance offshore 2 or 3 miles. At sunset we saw Gheria flag staff s b e. Saw several vessels at anchor off Gheria.

Wednesday 11 February

At 1.30 am the Admiral made the signal at which time we came to an anchor in 14 fathoms of water. At sunrise Gheria flag staff bore s e and Regapore island e b n. Distance offshore 3 or 4 miles. Found riding near the *Bridgewater* and *Kingfisher*, with the company's ships *Revenge*, *Protector*, *Guardian* and the Mahratta fleet[7], and saw standing in for this place h m s *Cumberland* and *Tiger*, the *Bombay* grab etc.

Thursday 12 February

Moderate sea and land breeze. At 2.30 pm a signal for the fleet to weigh and for the *Kingfisher* to run into the harbour with the *Bridgewater* (20 gun ship), the *Revenge, Bombay* grab and *Guardian*. In h m s *Tiger* (Captain Knowles) led. After them h m s *Kent* and *Cumberland* in which were the two Admirals and the *Protector* of 50 guns, in the rear bomb ketches etc. The fort fired very briskly on our fleet while we were standing into the harbour. At 4 pm we came to an anchor and the whole fleet began to engage, also the bomb ketches, the enemy firing as fast as they could on the whole fleet and the bomb ketches. At 4.30 pm a ten-inch shell from the *Triumph* prawn bomb ketch, commanded by Lieutenant Hetzler r a falling in amongst Angria's fleet set fire to one of their largest ships, which communicated to the rest of his ships, which set fire to most of his fleet (N B a great loss to the capturers). About 5.30 pm, a ten-inch shell from the *Drake* ketch commanded by Lieutenant Wood, R A, fell into a magazine of powder which blew up and set fire to the easternmost part of the Fort, which continued burning all night. At sunset the Admiral hauled down the red flag and left off firing, as also did the rest of the fleet, except the four bomb ketches which were to keep firing until further orders. At the same time Admiral Watson hove out the signal for all the boats in the fleet to be manned and armed and at 9.30 the troops were landed without any opposition, They had five men killed on board the *Cumberland,* four on board the *Tiger* and one on board the *Guardian*. About 11.30

[7] The plan was to take Gheria and hand it over to the Mahratta prince from whom Angria had seized it so the Mahrattas provided assistance by sea.

a shell from the *Drake* blew up another magazine in the westernmost part of the fort, which they extinguished in about $1\frac{1}{2}$ hours. At 12 a carcass was fired from the *Drake* which set fire to the westernmost part which continued burning until 5 the next morning. (NB the Mahratta never came within gun shot of the fort until such time as the fort was set on fire and then they hurried in their boats and landed their forces by 10 pm thinking that they should get the first possession of the fort.)

FRIDAY 13 FEBRUARY

At daylight we heard that Angria's fleet was entirely consumed, with several store houses etc. At 9 am the Admiral warped nearer the fort and also the *Tiger* and *Salisbury*. At the same time we were informed that Tologu Angria had offered terms and that they had opened the gates to our forces but on their march he fired on them, wounding an officer and killing a sergeant of the infantry and wounding several private men. Upon which the Admiral immediately sent a patamar [messenger] with a flag of truce to Angria to know if he would surrender up the fort, on which account we were all quiet until the return of the boat. At 12.30 the flag returned on board the *Kent*, on which we had a signal to weigh anchor and to go about 800 yards further up the river. About 3 pm we came to an anchor and again engaged the fort from the men of war and bomb ketches for about an hour when they waved a white flag at the fort, on which the Admiral made a signal to cease firing and sent his boat with a white flag. About 5 pm the boat returned, on which all the fleet began to fire very briskly until near sunset when they again waved the white flag on which a signal was made to leave off firing. At the same time the Admiral sent his boat on shore, and our forces marched up to the fort gates resolved to storm, but about 6.30 pm the fort surrendered. Our troops marched in and the English flag hoisted and Angria's colours hauled down, at which three cheers were given by all the fleet, but Angria had made his escape out of the fort. An Englishman whose name is Rice was taken in the fort and sent on board to the Admiral. He proved to be a deserter from the English about 8 years ago. He was made Angria's chief engineer. He says that Angria's forces were not above a thousand men, amongst which he had about 14 Europeans. The town was still on fire to the east (NB the number of forces on this expedition were five companies of artillery, 400 of infantry, 850 Sepoys, besides the Mahrattas – the latter of no service, only as a show).

SATURDAY 14 FEBRUARY

This morning Angria's troops marched out of the fort, except his wife, his two sons, two daughters, his brother and brother-in-law and servants who were all put in a house of security with three sentries over the house for fear they should receive any abuse from the soldiers. In the afternoon our troops marched into the fort. The sailors were employed in getting the guns out of Angria's grabs which were burnt, and carrying them on board the men-of-war.

SUNDAY 15 FEBRUARY

Our commissary with several others were employed in weighing the cash which was found in his treasury etc. The same day the Mahrattas were allowed to hoist their flag on one of the round towers in the eastern-most part of the town. The sailors employed as yesterday.

MONDAY 16 FEBRUARY

The two Admirals came on shore and were saluted by the fort with 23 guns. The men off duty were employed in attending the horses, elephants and cattle taken in the fort. The Mahrattas were not suffered to come into the fort until further orders, the men of war's men were employed in sundry things on shore. This day we were informed that Angria had delivered up all his forts along the sea coast to the Mahrattas. We found in the fort 90 horses, 5 elephants, one camel and several cows and goats.

TUESDAY 17 FEBRUARY

The artillery officers and men from the four bomb ketches ordered on shore to join their respective companies in the fort.

WEDNESDAY 18 FEBRUARY

Gheria. A fire happened this morning which burned several of the officers' quarters: the fort all in confusion, but by the assistance of soldiers and sailors with Indians from the men of war, we got it extinguished by night. The fatigue the fire occasioned to the officers by moving their baggage which lay contiguous to the conflagration laid several of them up; the place at present is very unwholesome by the disagreeable smoke ascending from the places that were set on fire before and also from this late fire, so that we are at present among smoke, rubbish and ruins.

THURSDAY 19 FEBRUARY

Employed in collecting the bale goods[8] and sending them on board the men of war and searching out for other treasure. This evening the *Tiger* and *Bridgewater* sailed from here bound for Bombay.

MONDAY 23 FEBRUARY

Received our field batta money from 27 February to 25 February which was to reach Captain and Captain/Lieutenant 6 rupees a day, Lieutenants 4, ensigns 3. The same day about twenty of Angria's servants were sent out, both men and women; about the quantity that was thought sufficient for the use of the family.

Tuesday, Wednesday and Thursday employed in collecting all the copper and guns together and sending the copper on board the men of war.

THURSDAY 26 FEBRUARY

Sailed from hence the *Kingfisher* sloop for Bombay, the same day we found a magazine of gun powder, which contained about a thousand barrels and chests. Looking out for more magazines of powder etc.

FRIDAY 27 FEBRUARY

Sold the five elephants to the Mahrattas for ten thousand rupees.

SUNDAY 29 FEBRUARY

This morning Lieutenant Bennet of the Company's artillery died. He was buried in the afternoon. Minute guns were fired on his being carried to the grave. Mr Newman, Volunteer, was made a Lieutenant by his vacancy, by Colonel Clive.

MONDAY 1 MARCH

Several men belonging to the Royal and Company's artillery taken with the smallpox, it being amongst Angria's family when we took the place. The Company was pleased to make a present of one hundred rupees to the artillery officers who had the command of the bomb ketches at the reduction of Gheria.

[8] Cotton, cloth etc.

TUESDAY 2 MARCH

Gheria. All those men that never had the smallpox were ordered to march out of the fort as there were barracks provided for them about 200 yards from the walls; the men off duty were busy in sorting the powder that was found in the magazines. The same day most of the horses that were taken in the fort were sold.

THURSDAY 4 MARCH

Lieutenant Grove of the R A with all the men that never had the small-pox embarked on board the *Protector* (Commodore James) for Bombay.

FRIDAY, SATURDAY & SUNDAY

Our men dying very fast with the smallpox. Lieutenant Nielsen of the company's artillery embarked with 30 men that never had the smallpox on the *Harwich* storeship for Bombay.

TUESDAY 9 MARCH

Embarked the three companies of the R A with some of the company's artillery. 360 infantry and 350 sepoys were left in Gheria. The same evening the *Bombay* grab arrived with Mr De La Garde, one of the council at Bombay, to act as Governor of Gheria and Captain Govin to act as Commandant of the troops there until it is known whether Gheria is to be delivered to the Mahrattas or the East India Company, or kept for the King's use.

WEDNESDAY 10 MARCH

This morning the *Bombay* grab saluted the Admiral which was returned the same evening; sailed the *Salisbury* with two or three more ships in company for Bombay.

THURSDAY 11 MARCH

This morning a signal for sailing and was all under sail by 7 am; left at Gheria, the *Bombay* grab and *Revenge* with several gallivats belonging to the company. Came in sight of Anti Gheria about 4 pm.

TUESDAY 16 MARCH

About 5 pm came in sight of Bombay and at 8 pm came to an anchor in 7 fathoms of water: at low water $4\frac{1}{2}$ fathoms.

WEDNESDAY 17 MARCH

At 10am the pilot came on board and at 1pm came to an anchor in the harbour in 4 fathoms: the *Kent* was in the day before, and disembarked Captain Skeddy's company RA.

THURSDAY 18 MARCH

About 6am Captain Maitland's company of RA disembarked from the *Cumberland*, the agents very busy in selling the prize goods brought from Gheria.

SATURDAY 20 MARCH

Came in the *Salisbury* and about 11am Captain Northall's company of RA disembarked.

MONDAY 22 MARCH

Came to an anchor the *Warrior* ketch with Captain Carter's company of artillery and Lieutenant Barrett of the King's artillery.

MONDAY 5 APRIL

Field day of the three companies of the RA and on this instance we had another Field day and went through the firings.

WEDNESDAY 14 APRIL

The *Drake* ketch came to an anchor. The next day we received part of our Gheria prize money which was to each Captain 2806 rupees, to each Lieutenant 1007, NCO's 320, Privates 56. Black soldiers received 20 rupees. The same day we received our Gheria field batta to the time of our landing at Bombay.

SATURDAY 17 APRIL

Bombay. A field day of our artillery and to be continued three times a week until further orders.

EASTER MONDAY 19 APRIL

This evening the 'Fair Penitent'[9] was acted by the gentlemen of the navy and army.

[9] A play by Nicholas Rowe; first acted in London 1703.

THURSDAY 27 APRIL

HMS *Kent, Cumberland, Tiger* and *Salisbury* sailed from here for Madras, in order to escape the monsoon which is expected in June. Saluted the Fleet from the fort with 17 guns which was returned.

11 MAY

The *Kingfisher* sloop (Captain Tovey) sailed from here with an express that came overland from England for Admiral Watson at Madras. This month excessive hot and sultry; our men dying very fast, having lost forty since we came to India.

JUNE 7

Bombay. The Monsoons (or periodical winds) began this day to set in, with thunder, lightning and heavy rains. Received our batta money as allowance in quarters for the Month of May. The NCOs and privates likewise received theirs and also the short allowance money whilst on their passage from England to the East Indies.

JUNE 14

Edward Hurst, sergeant, was broke to a mattross and received 400 lashes by order of a Regimental Court martial for striking Lieutenant Barrett of the RA.

JULY 11

Lieutenant George Campbell RA died at 3 am. He was buried the same evening. Lieutenant Grove with 24 men were the firing party. Sergeant Brereton made Lieutenant Fireworker by his vacancy.

JULY 17

The *Drake* ketch sailed from here bound for Gombroon (Bander Abbas) in Persia as a guard ship to the company's factory there.

JULY 23

The Sessions began here: the next day one of the black men was hanged for strangling a child.

JULY 26

The Sessions ended and brought in guilty one Gentoo to be hanged for stealing copper: one to lose his ears and to be pilloried and another to be whipped.

TUESDAY 3 AUGUST
The three companies of the R A were mustered.

TUESDAY 10 AUGUST
A ceremony performed here every year by the Brahmins (or priests) of different sects of religion, which is by throwing coconuts as far as they can into the sea as an offering to Neptune (God of the sea) to pacify the sea until the next monsoons, counting the monsoons for this year over; so that all ships are permitted to go out on their different voyages until the coming of the next.

SUNDAY 22 AUGUST
Mrs Bourchier, the Governor's lady, died this morning. Was interred the same evening in the Church; a funeral sermon preached by Rev. Doctor Howells.

WEDNESDAY 1 SEPTEMBER
Mustered the 3 companies R A. Seventy of our men died since our arrival. We have lately received accounts privately that the French are preparing a large fleet at the Mauritius: it is supposed in order to lay siege to Bombay, on which information all the troops off duty were told off to repairing the works and fortifications and making some additions.

FRIDAY 3 SEPTEMBER
Bombay. E I M *Portfield* (Captain Godfrey) from London came to anchor. On 6 the *Clinton* (Captain Nanson) came in and on 7th the *Royal Duke*, all coming from England.

MONDAY 13 SEPTEMBER
Messrs Spencer and Byfield, two of the Council, sailed from here: sent as ambassadors by the Governor to the Mahrattas to settle with them on some private affairs. They were saluted by the ships.

FRIDAY 17 SEPTEMBER
The *Edgecoat* (Captain Pierce) arrived from Macao. They lost two anchors and several bales of goods which they were obliged to throw overboard to lighten the ship.

SUNDAY 19 SEPTEMBER

About 1 am Hugh Simmons Esq, one of the Bombay councillors, died. He was buried this evening.

MONDAY 20 SEPTEMBER

The *Rose* galley (Captain Chandler) arrived from Madagascar and brought accounts that EIM *Dodington* which left England with us in 1755 struck a rock on 17 July 1755, and that there were only 23 people saved out of 276, on the coast of Africa, between the Cape of Good Hope and Madagascar. Those people that were saved got on a little island, made a boat from the wreck of the *Dodington* and sailed to Madagascar where Captain Chandler received them on board his ships. The 1st, 2nd, 3rd and 5th mates with 3 men of the King's artillery and 16 sailors were those saved.[10]

FRIDAY 1 OCTOBER

Bombay. We had the greatest quantity of thunder and lighting that was known by the inhabitants for these several years. EIM *Clinton's* main mast, main top mast, fore top mast, and main yard were split, and did damage to several other ships. The same day we had a muster of our three companies of artillery.

WEDNESDAY 6 OCTOBER

The *Warren* grab (Captain Phillips) arrived and brought the express from Basra of the Declaration of War being declared in London against the French on 17 May 1756.[11] The *Success* snow (Captain George) and the *Experiment* brigantine (Captain Brackford) arrived at the same time from Muscat.

THURSDAY 7 OCTOBER

All the troops were under arms this morning at 9 when the King's Declaration of War was read at the head of the troops by Master Daniel Draper, secretary to the Council. Three huzzas given by the troops.

---

[10] Three mattrosses of Hislop's company RA survived the shipwreck: John Linton, Ralph Smith and Edward Dyrog. See Shipwrecks and Disasters at Sea. Vol. 2 p. 320–349. Edinburgh 1812 and also *Gentleman's Magazine* 1756. Robert Clive lost £3000 in the ship.

[11] The fastest news came overland via Aleppo/Baghdad.

FRIDAY 8 OCTOBER

A patamar arrived from Bengal with news that Bengal was taken by the Moors and that the Governor and Council were taken and confined as prisoners. 146 confined in the Black Hole, 10 foot square – 23 survived and 123 died in one night.

MONDAY 18 OCTOBER

Mr Spencer and Mr Byfeld[12] who were sent some time ago to treat with the Mahrattas arrived. The same day the Hector (Captain Williams) arrived from Gombroon in Persia.

TUESDAY 19 OCTOBER

The Mahratta general came here and on his landing was saluted by the ships and also by the fort.

FRIDAY 22 OCTOBER

All the company's troops under arms and went through the platoon firing and the quick firing with the cannon before the Mahratta general.

SATURDAY 23 OCTOBER

Sailed from hence the *Bombay* grab. The same day Gheria was delivered up to the Mahrattas by order from the Council of Bombay, on which EIM *Royal Duke* sailed for Gheria in order to bring home the company's troops which were in garrison there. At the same time the Mahratta general took his passage on board her and on his embarkation he was saluted by the fort and the shipping.

THURSDAY 28 OCTOBER

Bombay. Two companies of infantry consisting of 200 men in each company, commanded by Captain Buchanan and Captain Armstrong with 60 of the company's artillery commanded by Captain Lieutenant Egerton, embarked for Bengal; the same day Lieutenant John Smith of the RA died.

FRIDAY 29 OCTOBER

Sailed from hence with the troops that embarked yesterday, the *Revenge* (Commodore James) with the *Arrixa* (Captain Roberts) and the *Mamada* (Captain Creton). This morning Lieutenant Smith was

[12] Members of the Bombay Presidency Council.

interred; 3 volleys were fired over his grave by 30 men under the command of Lieutenant Corbett. Mr George Elliot who was our commissary's assistant made a fireworker on the above vacancy.

TUESDAY 2 NOVEMBER
Some of the troops from Gheria arrived with news that the fort was delivered to the Mahrattas on 28 October. Angria's family was also delivered to the Mahrattas agreeable to their choice and the next day the remainder of our troops and ships arrived.

9 AND 10 NOVEMBER
Several large Portuguese ships came to an anchor here. They saluted the fort which was returned.

SATURDAY 20 NOVEMBER
Captain/Lieutenant Mason of the RA died and was buried the same afternoon. Lieutenant Whitmore had the firing party of 30 men. After interment the minute guns fired from the fort. First Lieutenant Whitmore made Lieutenant and Bombardier Davis Fireworker.

SUNDAY 16 JANUARY 1757
Bombay. About 1 pm Lieutenant Corbett of the RA died and was buried the next morning. Firing party of 30 men commanded by Lieutenant Grove fired three volleys over his grave.

TUESDAY 18 JANUARY
Lieutenant Daniel Grove of the company's troops was made a Lieutenant Fireworker on the above vacancy.

SATURDAY 5 FEBRUARY
A fire broke out withoutside of the Busar Gate near the Portuguese church and in about four hours consumed near 150 small houses and huts.

WEDNESDAY 9 FEBRUARY
Byculla. Marched from hence Captain Skeddy's with half of Captain Maitland's company and 8 officers for Byculla to practice with guns and mortars which were 12-inch and 8-inch mortars, one royal howitzer and one coehorn mortar, with one 12-pounder and two short sixes. The command was ordered by Major Chalmers to remain there a fortnight.

THURSDAY 10 FEBRUARY

Bombay. HMS *Triton*, 20 guns (Captain Townly) anchored. She left Woolwich 15 July 1756. Brought news that the French had landed their forces on the island of Minorca 20 April 1756, but that General Blakeney had not as yet given it up when he left England.

FRIDAY 25 FEBRUARY

Captain Northall's with the other half of Captain Maitland's company relieved the command at Byculla to practice with the guns and mortars there.

FRIDAY 11 MARCH

A party of the company's artillery relieved the party of the King's artillery at Byculla. The day before a fire broke out at Dungaree (Dongri) which in two hours consumed above 100 houses. The same day we received news that our forces had retaken Bengal from the Nabob.

SUNDAY 20 MARCH

A command of 50 of the company's infantry with Captain Lane and Lieutenant Dimond and one ensign with Councillor Spencer had embarked in one of the company's ships for Anjengo.

SATURDAY 16 APRIL

Bombay. The Sessions began and brought in three of the black men to be whipped and to be confined to hard labour for two years for robbing some of the poor inhabitants when their houses were on fire at Dungaree.

MONDAY 25 APRIL

The news of Bengal retaken by Admiral Watson and Colonel Clive was confirmed but that our forces that left this place on 28 October had not arrived when the place was taken. On this information Governor Bourchier gave an entertainment with a ball at night. Our forces there have settled a peace with the Nabob, and the company has liberty to build what fortifications they please in Bengal etc. 31 January 1757.

SATURDAY 7 MAY

Captain Skeddy was taken ill of a disorder in his bowels in the morning and died this evening. He was buried the next day. Captain Lieutenant Winter, Lieutenants Grove and Davis had the command of the firing party of 50 men with 2 sergeants, 2 corporals, 2 drummers and one fifer fired 3 volleys over his grave, and immediately after the minute guns fired from the fort. Captain/Lieutenant Tovey was made Captain and Lieutenant Sir Charles Chalmers Captain Lieutenant, Robert Hetzler First Lieutenant, John Chalmers 2nd Lieutenant and also Adjutant and Doctor Harling made Lieutenant Fireworker, dated from 9 November[13].

TUESDAY 10 MAY

Bombay. Mr Walker, commissary, is appointed to act as Quartermaster in the room of John Chalmers promoted to an adjutant. Very heavy rains with thunder and lightning which continued all night.

MONDAY 16 MAY

Received our second payment of Gheria prize money which was paid by Mr Mackay, secretary to the Admiral, which was to each Captain and Captain Lieutenant 706, Lieutenant 255, Sergeants 81, and privates 14 rupees each.

JUNE 3

HMS *Triton* sailed for Madras and Bengal in order to meet Admiral Watson and his squadron.

JUNE 10

This morning the monsoons set in with heavy rains, thunder and lightning.

FRIDAY 1 JULY

A patamar arrived with news that Admiral Watson with the *Tiger* and *Salisbury* with the land forces commanded by Colonel Clive, had taken Chandernagore, a French settlement in the taking of which they had lost several officers and men on 24 March 1757.

---

[13] Dr Harling had been surgeon on an EIM apparently. Later he was dismissed as an impostor and went over to the Mahrattas. Joined the Bengal Medical Service and perished in the Patna massacre of 1763.

MONDAY 18 JULY

The Sessions began and ended on 22nd when two Europeans were brought in guilty of death for house-breaking, and several others to be whipped. Heard that Colonel Clive had defeated Suraja Dowla, and made Jaffir Ali Khan Nabob.

WEDNESDAY 10 AUGUST

Bombay. The two Europeans that were condemned were hanged this morning and the others were whipped round Bombay town.

FRIDAY 12 AUGUST

Captain Mostyn's company of infantry arrived here from Bankot. Left an ensign with 50 sepoys there. By private accounts we hear that the French are making all the preparations imaginable in fitting out a fleet to attack Bombay, on which we have set all our spare hands to mend and strengthen our fortifications.

29 AUGUST

This day the ceremony of flinging the coconut was performed by the Brahmins, they counting the monsoons over.

2 SEPTEMBER

Several ships belonging to the French with six men of war seen from Tellicherry off Mahé; the men of war are supposed to be Indian ships, converted into men of war.

SUNDAY 9 OCTOBER

This morning at daylight four large ships were seen standing in for this place on which we sent a pilot boat, but they would not suffer the boat to come near them. The next morning all the troops were ordered under arms, and all the guns were loaded thinking they were really the French squadron, several of the inhabitants getting off the island as fast as they could.

MONDAY 10 OCTOBER

About 10 am we discovered them to be English, having hoisted their colours and about 2 pm they came to an anchor, viz: HMS *Elizabeth* of 70 guns, (Commodore Stevens and Captain Kempenfeldt) HMS *Weymouth* 60 guns (Captain Vincent), HMS *Yarmouth* 70 guns (Captain Frankland) and HMS *Newcastle* 50 guns (Captain Hutchinson). They left England last March with four companies of marines, the

Commodore sent the *Success* 20 guns (Captain Legg) to the other coast with expresses for Admiral Watson. Brought news of Admiral Byng being shot for neglect of duty in the Mediterranean off Mahon on 20 May 1756 and the loss of Minorca.

THURSDAY 13 OCTOBER
This morning Lieutenant George Elliot of the RA died. He was buried in the afternoon, a firing party of 30 men commanded by Lieutenant Brereton fired three volleys over his grave.

MONDAY 24 OCTOBER
Two black men and one black woman were hanged in chains for the murder of Mr Limgey a black merchant of this place.

MONDAY 31 OCTOBER
Mr Francis Wood, gentleman, was appointed Lieutenant/Fireworker in the room of Lieutenant Elliot.

15 NOVEMBER
Three of the company's ships arrived here from Tellicherry and Anjango. They brought news of the death of Admiral Watson who died of a fever at Bengal. The same evening a play was given to the gentlemen and ladies by the padres (or priests) at the back of the Portuguese church after which there was a cold collation.

24 NOVEMBER
This morning Lieutenant Munro of the marines died; a firing party of 30 men commanded by Lieutenant Brereton RA fired 3 volleys over his grave.

2 DECEMBER
8 officers and 37 privates belonging to Colonel Adlercron's regiment [39th Foot] arrived[14]. They came here to take their passage for England on account of the said regiment being ordered home. They left Madras the latter end of October but could not get a passage home from thence[15].

[14] Colonel Adlercron had brought the first King's Army Infantry Regiment to Madras in 1754 with a commission as C-in-C. Two further companies had come out in 1756.

[15] Some officers and many men of the 39th, "Primus in Indis" remained in India voluntarily when the Regiment was called home, transferring to the Company for a Bounty. Wood met those who opted to return home.

15 DECEMBER

Bombay. Doctor Gilbert Mathieson died suddenly of an apoplexy. He was buried the next morning. A captain's party fired 3 volleys over his grave and immediately after the minute guns fired.

24 DECEMBER

Captain Dick of the company's marine died. He was buried the next morning. A captain's party fired over his grave; minute guns were also fired immediately after his burial.

26 DECEMBER

Captain Frankland of HMS *Yarmouth*, 70 guns, died this morning. He was interred in the evening. A captain's party of the King's artillery did the duty and immediately after the minute guns fired.

27 DECEMBER

Four EI ships arrived viz: the *Lord Anson* (Captain Cheek) *Hawke*, (Captain Drake), *Latham* (Captain Foot) and the *York* (Captain Lascelles). Brought 100 of the King's artillery with 5 officers viz: Lieutenant George Phoenix, Agar Weetman, Thomas Pitts, Charles Wood and John Thiel. They left England on 2 June 1757 and brought 20 recruits for the Company's service and some sailors.

17 JANUARY 1758

Bombay. The detachment of artillery that arrived here last month embarked on board the four men of war in order to join Captain Hislop at Madras in the room of the artillery that were drowned in the *Dodington* in the year 1755.

21 JANUARY

The four men of war that arrived here last October in order to join Admiral Pocock on the other coast sailed. They saluted the Fort with 13 guns. Half an hour after they gave a royal salute of 21 guns to the shipping.

23 JANUARY

The *Prince Edward* EIM (Captain Halden) arrived from England, with the *Revenge* (Commodore James) from Bengal. A black man was hanged for the murder of his wife and child.

17 FEBRUARY

This morning Samuel Walker, Commissary, died. He was buried the same evening. Captain Whitmore, Lieutenant James Wood and Brereton with 50 men for the firing party; and a black man was hanged for robbery.

2 MARCH

Bombay. Our three companies of artillery were mustered by Edward Chandler esquire, who was appointed commissary in the room of Walker deceased, and Lieutenant Sweet was appointed Quartermaster to the RA by the above death.

8 MARCH

Embarked on board the *Revenge* and *Guardian*, Captain Forbes, Captain Heany, Lieutenant Nelson, Lieutenant Hamilton and Ensign Grant with 100 infantry and 20 gunners: all of the company's troops for a private expedition.

11 MARCH

Embarked on board the *Viper* ketch Lieutenant Smith of the Company's troops with 33 privates and 6 gunners for the above expedition.

16 MARCH

Orders for all the Royal Artillery, 6 companies of foot and 1200 sepoys to embark on Saturday morning. All the baggage to be sent on board on Friday for the above Surat expedition.

FRIDAY 17 MARCH

7 pm. The expedition is countermanded; the officers to send for their baggage, the commissarys and quartermasters to return their respective stores to their former magazines etc.

29 MARCH

Bombay. Major Chalmers has appointed Lieutenant Barrett to act as Captain/Lieutenant in the room of Captain/Lieutenant Whitmore, who is going to England, Lieutenant Groves as first Lieutenant and Lieutenant Sweet as second Lieutenant.

SUNDAY 9 APRIL
Sir James Foulis Bart, Major in the Company's infantry, and Major John Chalmers in the Royal Artillery, set sail in the *Prince Edward* (Captain Halden) bound for England.

MONDAY 10 APRIL
Embarked on board Captain/Lieutenant Whitmore, Captain J. de Funck, head engineer, Lieutenant Trombley, Lieutenant Kidswell and several other gentlemen in the Company's service, Lady Fowlis and her family, Mrs Buchanan and her family, all for England. Embarked also some of the gentlemen belonging to Adlercron's viz: Captain Hunt, Captain/Lieutenant Galley, Lieutenant Hewitson, Lieutenant Lewis and Ensign Cartwright with 18 privates. The ships bound for England: the *Prince Edward, Lord Anson* (Cheek) and *York* (Lascelles) all sailed this evening; they saluted the fort which was returned to each of the ships by the fort.

TUESDAY 11 APRIL
A command of 30 of the Company's artillery and two Lieutenants went to Byculla, to practice with guns and mortars.

WEDNESDAY 12 APRIL
Bombay. Captain Carter, Commandant of the Company's artillery, died this morning. He was buried in the evening with the usual ceremony

SUNDAY 16 APRIL
Mr George Twiddell one of the Company's writers died; a Lieutenant's command fired over his grave three volleys and the fort gave him 14 minute guns.

31 MAY
This evening the monsoon came in with heavy thunder, lightning and rain.

6 JUNE
A new ship belonging to Captain Hough was launched, called the *Patte* (Captain Dean commander). She is made to carry about 400 tons. On the occasion a genteel entertainment was given in the yard under sheds to the gentlemen and ladies.

11 JUNE

This morning Captain Hogg of the Company's artillery died and was buried in the evening with the usual ceremony.

20 JUNE

A patamar from Madras with accounts of an engagement between the French and our fleet in which our fleet was obliged to run two 20-gun ships on shore and the sailors of the said two ships reinforced Fort Saint Davids, the French having laid siege to it. The French ran a 64-gun ship on shore and the rest of the French fleet made the best of their way for Pondicherry. They lost about 600 men, and our fleet lost one Lieutenant and 28 sailors – Monsieur Comte d'Aché commodore of the French.

SATURDAY 1 JULY

This afternoon Counsellor Scott died of the measles. He was interred next morning in the churchyard. A captain's party fired over his grave and then the minute guns.

15 JULY

The Sessions began and ended on 19th. Two black men were condemned to be hanged, but one of them had his reprieve at the gallows. On 21 instant a woman was also condemned to be hanged.

TUESDAY 25 AND WEDNESDAY 26 JULY

The *Revenge* and *Drake* arrived from Persia with news that the Duke of Cumberland is divested of all his military employments, that Sir John Ligonier was made Captain General in his room[16], that Admiral Holborne and Hawke were taken in a gale of wind and obliged to throw most of their guns overboard. That General Mordaunt was under arrest for neglect of duty in regard to Rochefort, that the King of Prussia had beat an army belonging to the French consisting of 80,000 men[17], that his army only consisted of 35,000, that he had taken and killed above 30,000 and that Lord Loudoun was greatly distressed

---

[16] Cumberland resigned all his appointments after the Convention of Kloster-seven. Sir John Ligonier was made Commander in Chief.

[17] Frederick won the battle of Rossbach.

in North America;[18] that he has written to England for 10,000 men, and it is thought that if he does not speedily get them, he will resign, not being able to do anything with the forces he has now with him.

THURSDAY 27 JULY

A patamar arrived from Madras with accounts that the French had taken Fort Saint Davids. The siege lasted about a month, that our forces marched out with the honours of war, and a few days after, the French blew up the place, and it is thought they have a design to lay siege to Madras. They had, it's said, 4000 men when they laid siege to Fort Saint Davids and we but 800 in the Fort (May 1758). Admiral Pocock says that if three of his captains had done their duty when they attacked the French fleet, he would have routed them entirely, for which he has ordered two of them under arrest and the other he has sent home to England. According to the accounts the French lost 100 men at the siege; our troops lost but very few.

WEDNESDAY 9 AUGUST

Bombay. This morning the woman was hanged that was condemned last sessions. The same day a woman was drowned in a well at Mazagon by accident.

15 AUGUST

This morning Captain Morgan of the Company's Marine died and was buried. In the evening a Captain's party fired over his grave and then the minute guns.

SUNDAY 18 AUGUST

The ceremony of flinging the coconut into the sea was performed by the Brahmins, it being full moon, which is always observed in performing this ceremony.

22 SEPTEMBER

This morning First Lieutenant Hussey died. He was buried in the evening; firing party of 30 men commanded by Lieutenant Davies fired over his grave. He was made a First Lieutenant in England October 1755. Lieutenant John Scott made Second Lieutenant.

[18] Loudoun had failed to attack Louisburg.

MONDAY 2 OCTOBER

No First Lieutenant made and Mr John Plenderleith is appointed Lieutenant by Captain Maitland by the above death. The same day we had accounts from Surat of the death of Captain Galleard, Commandant of the Company's artillery, who went to Surat for his health.

8 NOVEMBER

The EIM *Latham* (Captain Foot) sailed this morning for England. Captain Armstrong of the Company's infantry with Mrs Hough, Mrs Scott and Mrs Almo and their families all bound for England.

11 NOVEMBER

Bombay. This morning a large fleet of ships was seen at sea; on which there was orders to beat to arms immediately and the guards at the gates to be doubled but when the ships came nearer we found them to be only the Portuguese Fleet which came to an anchor here.

15 NOVEMBER

Two men of war and six Indiamen anchored here, who left England on 7 March; they were bound for Madras, but they had such a long passage, and being the time of monsoons setting in on that coast, they were obliged to bear away from Goa for this island: viz: the *Grafton* of 70 guns (Captain Tiddeman), the *Sutherland* of 60 guns (Captain Grant), the Indiamen the *Rhode* (Macknamara), *Shaftesbury* (English), the *Winchelsea* (How), the *Britannia* (Blewet), the *Tilbury* (Manwairing) and the *Prince of Wales* (Captain Roberts) with between 500 or 600 of Lieutenant-Colonel Draper's regiment which was designed for Madras: the next day they disembarked and came to the barracks[19].

17 NOVEMBER

This morning the Portuguese fleet sailed from hence; saluted Captain Tiddeman with 13 guns which was returned by his ship with 11 guns.

25 NOVEMBER

Bombay. The two Admirals, Pocock and Stevens, with their fleet from Bengal and Madras, came to an anchor here, viz: HMS *Yarmouth* (Pocock and Captain Harrison) 70 guns, HMS *Elizabeth*, 70 guns (the

[19] 79th Regiment – raised by Colonel William Draper (1st Guards) for service in India. later sent to the Philippines.

Commodore and Captain Kempenfeldt), HMS *Cumberland,* 66 guns
(Captain Kirk) HMS *Tiger,* 60 guns (Latham), HMS *Weymouth,* 60 guns
(Summerset), HMS *Newcastle,* 50 guns (Colville), HMS *Salisbury*
(Brereton) HMS *Queensbury,* 20 guns (Captain Digby Dent): eight men
of war: they left the *Kent,* 70 guns, at Bengal, she being unfit for
service, formerly Admiral Watson's ship but now condemned: brought
news of a sea engagement off Pondicherry between the two fleets on
3 August but night coming on, the French made their escape.
Commodore Stevens wounded as also Captain Martin: the French
sailed for Isle of Bourbon to refit, 540 French and 40 English killed [3
August 1758].

11 DECEMBER
One of the private men belonging to the Company was to be shot this
day by the sentence of a general court martial; composed of their own
officers – on which all the Company's troops were under arms at the
place of execution and a Captain's guard marched with the prisoner,
beating the dead march to the place where he was to be shot, and the
men who were to fire called out for that purpose; but his reprieve was
sent from the Governor which was read by Adjutant George Chalmers
of the Company's troops.

SATURDAY 16 DECEMBER
Bombay. Lieutenant-Colonel Draper's regiment embarked in order to
sail for Madras with the greatest expedition; they were all in good
health when they went on board.

SUNDAY 17 DECEMBER
This morning Captain Maitland of the Royal Artillery was married to
Miss Southby and also Captain Northall of the said detachment to Miss
Rumbolt. The same day sailed five Indiamen (with the troops that
embarked yesterday); viz: the *Tilbury, Prince of Wales, Shaftesbury,
Winchelsea, Britannia,* and HMS *Queensborough,* 20 guns with the EI
Revenge, 20 guns (Commodore Cable) as a convoy for the above ships
for Madras.

THURSDAY 21 DECEMBER
Lieutenant Balfour of Colonel Adlercron's regiment died this
morning[20]. He came here in one of the men of war in order to get his

[20] Balfour, originally a cadet in the RA, had evidently sailed with the RA
detachment accompanying the 39th Regt.

passage from this place to England; a firing party commanded by Lieutenant Davis fired over his grave.

TUESDAY 12 JANUARY 1759
Bombay. EIM *True Britain* (Captain Creton) and the *Drake* (Fisher) arrived from England; the men on board very sickly; brought 120 recruits for the Company's service.

22 JANUARY
The Session, begun and ending on Thursday 24 instant, brought in six to be hanged; three for murder, three for house breaking and several to be whipped around the town.

27 JANUARY
Two Europeans and one black man was hanged for murder and their bodies were given to the surgeons according to their sentence last Session. EIM *Admiral Watson* arrived from England bringing some recruits for the Company's service.

7 FEBRUARY
Embarked on board the *Bombay* grab (Captain Clough) and the *Fox* ketch (Captain Nisbett) 150 Europeans and topasses under the command of Captain Lane and Captain Forbes for a special expedition (supposed for Surat). Received our third and last payment of Gheria prize money.

THURSDAY 8 FEBRUARY
[*See plate 44*].
To Surat. This morning the following ships were ready to take in troops for an expedition under the command of Captain Maitland RA, viz: the *Guardian* (Captain Good), the *Protector* (Captain Creton), the *Dragon* (Captain Attenborough), *Patta Dolla* grab (Captain Jones), with 4 bomb ketches viz: *Drake* (Captain Baily) 10-inch mortar, the *Triumph* prawn (Cresier) 10-inch mortar, *Success* (Lindsey) 8-inch mortar and the *Defence* (Scott) 8-inch mortar. Captain Barrett RA commanded the ketches with an officer on board each. Lieutenant James Wood, the *Drake*, Lieutenant Hetzler RA the second, Lieutenant Hamilton the third, and Lieutenant Nielsen the fourth. The troops that embarked today with those that embarked on 7 January were Europeans and topasses, with 1500 sepoys, 216 of the Royal Artillery and 102 of the Company's artillery and 100 lascars to act as labourers.

Friday 9 February

Were all under sail by 10 am with a pleasant land breeze in company with the *Sutherland* (Captain Grant) man of war, 60 guns, three gallivats and about 70 boats but the wind being against us we were obliged to come to at every tide; the current being so rapid we could make no way, though several trials but all in vain so that we did not get to Surat Bar until

Thursday 15 February

Surat. Came to an anchor near Surat Bar; found several ships at anchor viz: Dutch, Danes, Portuguese and English; saluted the *Sutherland* with 11 guns: the lascars, sailors and soldiers employed in getting the guns and heavy stores out in order for the ships to get up the river. The *Bombay* grab and *Fox* ketch which sailed the 7th only crossed the bar yesterday in order to get up the river. It was very unfortunate we could not get here two days sooner, being two days after the spring tides, which put us to a great many inconveniences and hard labour. HMS *Newcastle* of 50 guns (Captain Colville) came to an anchor here. Two ketches with several boats under sail this evening in order to cross the Bar.

Friday 16 February

Getting the 10 inch mortar and stores out of the *Drake* ketch and got them on board the *Fox* ketch as she draws less water; it being impossible to get the *Drake* up but on the spring [tide]. It is 20 miles from the Bar to Surat which gave our enemies time to erect batteries.

Saturday 17 February

Surat. Getting our troops and stores out of the ships and embarking them on board the boats etc.

Sunday 18 February

Landed our troops and stores at a place called Gundelore [Dentilory] about 7 miles from Surat; the soldiers employed pitching their tents; mounted a main guard, quarter guard, picquet guard and sent out advanced parties etc.

Monday 19 February

Mr Spencer, Councillor and Chief Commandant, came on shore from on board the *Bombay* grab. Saluted by the gallivats. The *Success* and two ketches with some of the gallivats sailed a little way up the river and came to anchor near a place called Humbrah [Umra]

TUESDAY 20 FEBRUARY

All the army marched by 4 am in order to get nearer Surat: a more convenient ground and better water, but marching too near the outward walls of the town and within random shot of the enemy's cannon they fired on us, killing three or four sepoys and wounding several more. We retreated and marched to Humbrak or Humbrah, which was nearer the river and at low tide fresh water. Captain Northall R A died today, it is supposed through fatigue and heat of the sun. Several of our officers are very ill, the weather being so excessive hot. The troops lay on their arms all night as the boats were not come up with their tents and the bomb ketches endeavouring to get up the river. Several of the Swiss soldiers deserted this night.

WEDNESAY 21 FEBRUARY

Surat. For the future the roll is to be called five times a day in the presence of a subaltern. The army pitching their tents and getting their baggage on shore. Eleven more of the Swiss deserted, supposedly to the Dutch[21]; Captain Lieutenant Winter made Captain, Lieutenant Lewes Captain, Lieutenant Chalmers First Lieutenant, and Lieutenant Fireworker James Wood Second Lieutenant by the death of Captain Northall.

THURSDAY 22 FEBRUARY

Our officers and men pretty well recovered. Several more of the Swiss etc. deserted. We hear that Captain Grant of H M S *Sutherland* died at Surat Bar.

FRIDAY 23 FEBRUARY

A council of war was called by order of Captain Maitland, the opinion of which was to begin regular approaches and to erect batteries of 24-pounders to penetrate the walls while the 4 bomb ketches were working up the river with the *Bombay* grab and gallivats, on which embark 400 sepoys with the engineer for that duty: that is 200 with arms to cover the other 200 whilst at work in the trenches.

---

[21] The E I authorities had not kept the Swiss together as a company unit as promised, but dispersed them. Hence some discontent.

Saturday 24 February

Surat. Mr Samuel Court is appointed aide-de-camp to Captain Maitland and Mr Robert Scoon to hold rank as Lieutenant in the Company's troops. Orders for all the cooks to dress this day's and tomorrow's provisions, having orders this evening to march nearer Surat. Several more of our troops last night and this night deserted. The men employed in erecting batteries agreeable to yesterday's orders.

Sunday 25 February

This evening our troops moved their camp to near the Dutch Gardens and within gunshot of Surat, and this tide the *Triumph* prawn and *Defence* ketches got within bombarding range of Surat; the *Bombay* grab was not as yet so high.

Monday 26 February

At 4 am the enemy began firing from the French Gardens, which was returned with success for we marched up to the Gardens and took possession after exchanging several platoons' fire: Lieutenant Scoon wounded in his side; a few of our privates killed and several wounded. We then erected a battery of two short sixes made with bales of cotton on a hill a small distance from the town wall. In the meantime they fired several round shot against us; our battery being finished, we returned their fire doing some execution but our pieces being so short set the bales of cotton on fire several times. However, it was always easily extinguished by having plenty of water near the battery, and our people in high spirits in the night got two 24-pounders, a 13-inch mortar and coehorn up the hill to our battery and repaired the battery with sandbags and earth which occasioned our men to be very busy all night.

Tuesday 27 February

Surat. This morning the *Triumph* prawn and *Fox* ketches with two 10-inch mortars, fired on our enemies in the English Garden, Chelaby's Garden and on the English Bunder, the coehorn on shore firing at the Sidee's[22] grabs. At the same time we kept firing from our battery with the 24-pounders in order to make a breach in the town wall and now

---

[22] Sidee Ahmad Khan held from the Mogul Emperor of India the hereditary offices of Admiral and Governor of Surat. He was at odds with the Mahratta Chiefs. The various European Company factories and local merchants in Surat wanted order reestablished by the EIC who sent a force to oust the Sidees.

and then a few shells from the 13-inch mortar fell into the castle of
Surat which we continued all night. The enemy returned fire but very
slowly. Lieutenant Scoon died of the wound he received yesterday.

WEDNESDAY 28 FEBRUARY

Surat. This morning the enemy began cannonading much brisker than
the day before from the castle and batteries which they had lately
erected. However, we at last made a breach in the wall, at which a
storming party was ordered but was repulsed after several shot fired
on both sides, the breach being not sufficiently wide, and also a dry
ditch to get over. On this attack we lost Captain Funge, a brave officer
in the Company's service with Captain Jones who belonged to one of
the Company's ships, who turned out a volunteer. Lieutenant Gleets
was wounded in the neck, some few of the infantry killed and several
wounded; the same day a detachment under the command of
Lieutenant Francis Wood RA was sent on board the *Bombay* grab; a
sergeants' party on board the *Success* and the same number on board
the *Defence*.

THURSDAY 1 MARCH

About 10 am a party of about 200 Europeans and topasses with 800
Sepoys were ordered to embark in small boats in order to storm their
batteries within the walls of the town when the signal should be given
from the *Bombay* grab. At 3 pm she came, attended by the *Success* and
Defence with six gallivats and got up to the chain which the Sidees had
across the river as fast as possible. But the alarm being given in the
town they began to fire vigorously from all their batteries and also
from the castle; in all about 50 pieces of cannon; we firing as briskly
on them with our two 24-pounders, two twelves and two sixes, one
13-inch mortar, one royal howitzer and two coehorns, with two 10-
inch and one 8-inch mortars from the bomb ketches and all our guns
from our shipping. The cannonading continued with the
bombardment until 9 am when the signal was thrown out from the
Bombay grab, for the forces to make the attack. Immediately Captains
Lane, Forbes, English and Henry, with Lieutenants Bowyer, Dagon,
James Wood, Nielsen, Cockey, Francis Wood and Plenderleith, with
ensigns Harlow and Peppard, being all ready in the boats with the
troops that was ordered this morning, got off and rowed with the
utmost expedition across the river and under cover of our ships, being
against tide, then made another attempt to cross the river though
greatly exposed to their cannon from the Castle. However, we got
across the river and under their cannon ran our boats in as far as we

could, but not as far as we could wish, and so were obliged to jump out of our boats though up to our middles in mud and water. We then engaged with our small arms for about half an hour, causing them to retreat in great numbers, whereupon our ships and the troops from our batteries huzza'd our troops in pursuit of the enemy. Some of the detachment, with Commodore Watson of the company's fighting ships at their head, pursued the enemy for about three miles up the country. On coming back they dismounted several pieces of their cannon, broke open the main gate which had a rampart of earth behind it, and mounted a main guard. In the evening orders came from camp for our detachment to be on our guard within the walls as they had information that 7 or 8000 of the Sidees were to surprise us in the night. So informed we lay on our arms all night with advanced guards and out-sentries to give the signal of 'All's well' etc. Nothing material happened during the whole night except a false alarm. We lost in the landing Captain Inglis who was shot, some suppose by our own troops, Ensign Peppard wounded, with several privates killed and wounded on board and in landing.

FRIDAY 2 MARCH

Sidee's Bunder [pier]. We heard this morning that the Sidees had actually come from the Castle as far as the inner wall, but on some misunderstanding or because their courage failed, which is not known, they returned again into the town. Our people employed in bringing the gun and mortar stores into the main gate in order to be ready for the batteries. About 10 pm Captain Forbes with a party of 150 Europeans and topasses and 200 Sepoys went to cover the engineers with a party of artillery and ammunition, two short 6-pounders, cotton bales, entrenching tools, labourers etc. in order to erect a battery against the walls. Unfortunately this party missed the ground that was fixed on this morning so the above command returned about 1 am the next morning.

SATURDAY 3 MARCH

Sidee's Bunder. This morning we got our guns and mortars on shore from the ketches. The same party that went out yesterday went to cover the engineers in erecting the batteries that was proposed last night against the inner walls of Surat. About 9 am another party of 100 men under the command of Captain Heany, Lieutenant James Wood and Lieutenant Koetteritz, with a 6-pounder and a royal howitzer and 400 Sepoys to be in readiness to march into the town if occasion should offer, who proceeded almost under the walls and came to a halt, while a party of Sepoys with Captain Maitland and Commodore Watson went almost round the outward part of the inner walls. At length they returned and Captain Heany's party received orders to march back again. Several expresses came from the Governor, but not coming to an agreement about the delivery of the Castle, orders were given for a bombardment. We fixed our bomb battery at about 1100 yards from the Castle. About 6 pm we began to fire from the 13-inch and two 10-inch mortars which we continued until 2 am the next morning. In that time we blew up a magazine of powder and beat down part of one of their round towers. This put the Sidees in such a terror that they did not so much as fire one shot at us all night.

SUNDAY 4 MARCH
Sidee's Bunder. At 2 am orders were sent to cease firing by 3 when a party marched off the parade in order to secure one of the gates of the town having received information it was to be left open by some of our friends there. But before we had come up to the gate the enemy received notice of our intention and sent out from the castle a large command to the gate and drove out about 150 of their own sepoys. Then shut the gates and secured it by placing a large guard there. The party which they turned out joined our sepoys. At 8 am an express came from Mr Erskine belonging to our English factory at Surat, to Mr Spencer asking us not to fire our mortars but to give the Sidees two or three hours in order to consider on what terms they would deliver us the Castle. At about 11 am they sent word that the gates of the town were opened and that we might march in when we pleased. At which Captain Tovey R A was sent with a large command to secure the gate and place sentries on the walls. About 12 noon the whole marched into the town without any opposition; the streets were lined by thousands of the inhabitants who seemed to be rejoiced at our entrance into the town. We came to halt near our factory, and sent a messenger to the Governor to deliver up the castle. Several messages sent back and forward which occasioned a great delay, in which time one of the Sidees passed between our guard of sepoys and stabbed Lieutenant Hamilton with a kris or dagger in the thigh and endeavoured to make his escape, but one of our sergeants ran him through the body with his halberd. Several of our sepoys were killed by the Sidees shooting at them through the windows. At last an express was sent to the Governor of the Sidees that if he did not give orders to put a stop to such proceedings we would set their houses on fire and put everyone we found to the sword. After that we were pretty

quiet, but was obliged to secure a party of the Sidees in a house and planted a Captain's guard over them, securing ourselves in the best manner we could by planting guns and howitzers loaded with grape up their streets and lanes, and also opposite the places where we had any suspicion of their lurking. They being so tedious in the delivering up of the Castle, began to cause a murmur amongst the soldiers, and in particular as night was drawing on, surrounded by thousands of enemies, occasioned us all to be uneasy. At last the agreements were settled: the Castle to be delivered to the English on these conditions: to let the Sidees march out with their arms and accoutrements and to have all their household furniture secured for them, which was agreed, on which they marched out, and we marched in and by 8 pm we had the command of the Castle. We placed a main guard and secured the gates.

MONDAY 5 MARCH

Surat Castle. Fired the morning gun and beat the reveille at sunrise; fired a salute of 21 guns, at the same time hoisted the English colours on which all the ships that had guns saluted the colours; the Sidees getting their things out of the Castle agreeable to yesterday's orders. Mounted a Captain's guard and sent a Captain's guard to relieve Captain Tovey's guard at the main gate. About 12 noon Mr Spencer came on shore and was saluted by the ships; at 1 pm he passed by the Castle and was saluted with 21 guns. A general invitation by Mr Spencer to all the gentlemen to breakfast, dine and sup with him at the factory, while we remained in Surat. There will be coaches sent every day to the Castle for that purpose, as the Castle is about a mile from the factory. Getting all our guns and stores from the late batteries and relieving the outposts. Found in the Castle 173 brass and iron guns, two 10-inch brass mortars, with one royal howitzer and several thousand shot and shells, and several large magazines of powder and corn; a great number of stores of different natures etc. There was on the outward wall of the town about 240 pieces of cannon but very few on the inner wall. We found in the river belonging to the Sidees one large ship, one large three-mast grab, carrying 16 guns, and three smaller grabs, with 14 gallivats, several boats and great quantities of marine stores, anchors etc. NB We lost at this stage, by land 3 Captains, 1 Lieutenant, 1 Volunteer and 73 Privates, and about 50 sepoys – wounded 3 Lieutenants, 1 Volunteer, 30 privates and 40 sepoys. Deserted 1 Lieutenant, and about 200 Europeans, but mostly foreigners, and a few topasses with about 150 sepoys. As to the number of Sidees killed and wounded we could never learn, but its supposed we killed a great number, especially in the morning of the attack on the Sidee's Bunder, as several carts were seen by some of our factory at Surat full of dead bodies in order to be buried in their own ground. It is supposed that the taking of this place will be worth 50,000 rupees a year to the Company after repairing the castle and making a covered way and glacis.

TUESDAY 6 MARCH
Surat Castle. Captain Tovey RA is to be Commandant of the Castle and to be received by the Castle guard once a day with rested arms and to give him a ruffle with the drum. All other guards to turn out as often as he passes. Many employed clearing the rubbish: a party ordered to survey the guns, and another party to get the shot and shells together, for which the men were paid and the officer 2 rupees per day.

WEDNESDAY 7 MARCH
Surat Castle. Some of our soldiers made a disturbance in the town at which none was allowed out of the Castle without leave from the Commandant and a captain of the day was appointed and a Captain's guard ordered at the Castle gate and patrols to walk the streets every two hours from the guard to prevent quarrels.

SATURDAY 10 MARCH
Still at work in the Castle in clearing the rubbish and pulling down some of the shattered buildings occasioned by the bursting of our shells when the Castle was besieged; looking out for powder magazines, as likewise for shot and shells. Discharging the guns which we found loaded and also surveying the guns. Mr Spencer settling the affairs of Surat with the black merchants of Surat etc. A party of infantry commanded by Lieutenant Bowyer was ordered to embark on board one of the Company's ships there.

SUNDAY 11 MARCH
This morning the Royal Artillery went through their manual exercise. A great number of sailors employed in raising one of the Sidee grabs which they sunk the day we took their bunder. Our people in tolerable good health and our wounded recovering very fast. Mr Spencer made an agreement with the late Governor of the Sidees for buying all the stores belonging to the Castle to which he agreed.

TUESDAY 13 MARCH

Surat Castle. Captain Maitland has appointed Captain Lieutenant Black to command the late Captain Inglis's company and Lieutenant White to be a Captain/Lieutenant in the room of Captain Black. We had an account of two EIM, the *Edgecoat* and *Stretham* (Evans and Mason), seven months on passage. They brought 120 recruits for the Company's service. Captain Somerset and Michie belonging to HM's ships came on shore, where they were received by Mr Spencer.

THURSDAY 15 MARCH

Putting up the shot and shells in regular piles. About 4 pm hoisted the Mogul's colours[24] on one of the towers to the westward of the Castle and fired 11 guns as a salute to the colours. The next day Captain Maitland appointed Mr Moffett, gentleman, one of our volunteers, a Lieutenant in the RA. The Captain of the day taken off duty.

MONDAY 19 MARCH

The men who mount guard are to perform the parade motions before the guard is formed every morning. We finished the survey of guns and completed the shot and shells. Opened the sally port of the Castle to get in two 24- and two 12-pounders and one 13-inch with a 10- and 8-inch mortar to be left in the castle. Getting our field pieces on board with stores etc.

WEDNESDAY 21 MARCH

Surat Castle. News arrived here from Bombay of General Lally's raising the siege of Madras and that our troops had pursued them and taken several prisoners, cannon etc; at which information a salute of 21 guns was fired from the Castle. Captain Heany, Lieutenant Mason and 100 men embarked in small boats for Surat Bar in order to embark on board the *Protector* there and to wait for further orders. The next day 71 more of the infantry embarked on board the gallivats. Affairs are not quite finished between Mr Spencer and the black merchants. A party of the Mahrattas, both horse and foot, for these three days past has been seen about the outward walls of Surat, and has also stopped provisions coming into the town. A messenger was sent who returned with the answer that the merchants of Surat were indebted to them for two lakhs of rupees and that they insist on being paid.

---

[24] The EIC had the agreement of the Mogul to take on the office of Admiral and Governor of Surat as his tributary.

MONDAY 26 MARCH

A park line was ordered on each side of the Castle by Captain Tovey, and he got 14 guns mounted and loaded with grape shot. We pulled down a large chokey[25] and cut down several trees which was before the Castle gate. Affairs are not yet settled between the black merchants and the Mahrattas; the labourers are still employed in pulling down and clearing the Castle of the rubbish from the shattered buildings.

SATURDAY 31 MARCH

Surat Castle. About 2 am a fire happened in the Castle and near the large magazine of powder which occasioned an alarm but by the assistance of our people it was soon extinguished without any harm. This evening one of the Company's European soldiers happened to put his hand into the tiger's cage at the castle in order to stroke him as several had done before, but the brute caught hold of his hand and tore it in such a miserable condition that it had to be cut off above his elbow. The officer's guard at the town gate was relieved by a guard of Sepoys viz: one subadar, one jemadar, two havildars, two naicks and 46 sepoys, who are to remain at Surat. The next day the guard of the garrison was relieved by the troops which were to remain at Surat, and the Castle gate guard which consisted of a Captain's guard was relieved by a subaltern's guard.

WEDNESDAY 4 APRIL

Captain Forbes, Turner and Burr, with Lieutenants Hetzler and Grove, embarked this morning and sailed for the Bar in order to embark on board the ships waiting there to sail for Bombay with the troops that embarked a few days ago.

FRIDAY 6 AND SATURDAY 7 APRIL

Captains Barrett and Dean, Lieutenants Grove and Francis Wood, 2nd Lieutenant McKay and Ensign Harlow embarked for the Bar with the Nabob of Cambay in order to sail for Bombay.

TUESDAY 10 APRIL

Surat Castle. Captain Maitland's and Captain Tovey's companies of RA with the company's artillery embarked on board the boats at the Castle in order to sail for the Bar where they embarked on board the

---

[25] A Hindu word for police station: hence English equivalent 'chokey' – lock-up.

Bombay grab (Captain Clough). Orders for Captain Winters' company with the remainder of the Company's troops to embark on board the *Drake* and EIM *Fisher* as soon as the cotton is loaded on board which the said ship came to Surat for.

THURSDAY 12 APRIL

Captain Maitland was saluted with 13 guns on his embarking on board the *Bombay* grab. The *Drake* and *Defence* ketches sailed this evening for Bombay with several of our troops. The same evening an accident happened on board the *Dragon* (Captain Attenborough) by the main yard falling down which killed one man and wounded nine more.

FRIDAY 13 APRIL

By 11 am we were under sail in company with the *Dragon* (bound for Persia and two other vessels). About 12 midnight the *Dragon* etc left us near abreast of St John's. The next morning at 7 am we came in sight of Bassein and got up with the *Drake* and his convoy. In the evening came to an anchor, the tide being down.

SUNDAY 15 APRIL

Early this morning weighed anchor and sailed with a pleasant breeze and came to an anchor in Bombay Road about 5 pm. A little after Captain Maitland with some more of the officers disembarked. Saluted him with 13 guns from the *Bombay* grab, and also from Bombay Fort with the same number on his landing; had an account that the men of war had left Bombay on 9 April for Madras and confirmation of General Lally's raising the siege at Madras and that the two European ships viz: *True Briton* (Creton) and the *Admiral Watson* packet (Captain Cook) sailed for England a few days ago.

SATURDAY 21 APRIL

This morning the *Drake* EIM arrived with Captain Winters' company and the remainder of the Honourable Company's troops. The forces disembarked about 12 noon and marched to the parade where they were dismissed and sent to their respective quarters. Left in the Castle of Surat to do duty there were Captains Crosby, Degloss (Captain of Engineers) and Captain Batty, with Lieutenants Dagon, Nielsen, Cockey, Hewson and Walch with Ensign Scott, seven sergeants, six drummers and 100 rank and file, fifty of their artillery with one Tindal and 49 lascars as labourers for mounting and dismounting guns etc and likewise about 200 sepoys. Expedition of Surat over – a success.

4 MAY

Bombay. The *Drake* EIM (Captain Fisher) sailed for England by the way of China. Mr Sedgwick (one of the council here) with his wife took their passage for England on board her.

10 MAY

The EIM *Eastoak* (Captain Evans) sailed for England, with 12 passengers on board amongst which was Lieutenant Grove RA who had leave to go home for his health. The same evening she sprung two planks which obliged her to come back for repair. The next day Captain/Lieutenant Turner of the Company's artillery who was one of the passengers died. By 12th she was repaired and sailed.

16 MAY

A patamar arrived by the way of Persia with news that Louisburg the capital of the island of Cape Breton in North America and St John's was taken by the English under the command of Admiral Boscawen, Generals Amherst, Wolfe and Lawrence on 27 July 1758, and that Goree and Senegal in Africa was taken by the English under the command of Keppel and Colonel Worge on 1 May 1758: also that the French had been obliged to quit Hanover, which they had taken last year in opposition to Duke of Cumberland and his army, but by the intrepidity of the inhabitants, Hessians and Brunswickers under the command of Prince Ferdinand of Brunswick, they were entirely driven out and a great many of their army taken prisoner.

SUNDAY 27 MAY

Captain Mostyn died last night. He was buried at 6 pm. A captain's party of the company fired as usual and immediately after internment the minute guns fired.

THURSDAY 31 MAY

At 10.30 am a mattross in the company's service was shot for desertion.

SUNDAY 3 JUNE

The *Diligence* schooner (Captain McClashing) which left England in November 1758 arrived here bringing expresses for Admiral Pocock and a Flag to Commodore Stevens with confirmation of the English taking Louisbourg, and also the destroying of the famous pier and the ships in the harbour of Cherbourg, Normandy, in France. It was notified that 20 EIM ships were to come out this year with a great number of recruits for the Company's service. The expedition to Cherbourg was commanded by General Blyth and Commodore Howe. The Duke of York went as a volunteer with Howe in August 1758, and that several other places were taken by the English. The allied army under the command of Prince Ferdinand of Brunswick had engaged the French army commanded by the Prince de Clermont and Count de St Germain, near Crefeld, on 23 June, which began at 10 am with a continual fire on both sides until near 6 pm when the French gave way and retreated into the country of Cologne. The success of the battle was very much owing to the cannon. The enemy loss was about 6000 men killed, wounded and taken prisoner. They left in the field some standards and colours, as well as baggage and several pieces of cannon. Prince Ferdinand immediately laid siege to Dusseldorf, and in a few days obliged them to give up the place. Prisoners were not to carry arms for the space of one year against the allies.

MONDAY 4 JUNE
Bombay. Mr Chandler, commissary to the RA, is appointed by Captain Maitland a Lieutenant Fireworker in the RA[26]. Count L'Estaing taken prisoner in the sally.

6 JULY
A ship called the *Patta Salom* (Captain Simmons) arrived here with a confirmation of General Lally's raising the siege of Madras. He opened his batteries on 6 January 1759. A grand sally was made by Colonel Draper in which many officers and a great number of men were killed on both sides. On 16 February a reinforcement of 600 men belonging to Colonel Draper's regiment arrived from England, which were immediately landed, and that night Lally thought proper to draw off his forces, and made his retreat to Arcot leaving 40 pieces of cannon in the field. The defence of the place was carried on by the orders of Colonel Lawrence and Draper, Major Brereton and Caillaud and Mr Pigot, Governor. A complete victory was gained over the French in the neighbourhood of Masulipatam by Colonel Forde, commandant of the troops at Bengal in February 1759[27]. Captain Simmons also

[26] This appointment was never confirmed: clearly an unsatisfactory officer.

[27] Though the French were beaten back from Madras in February, it was not in fact until early April that Forde finally triumphed at Masulipatam – "this daring and marvellous adventure" – which overthrew French power in the Deccan and Northern Circars.

brought accounts of 13 sail of French men of war of the line with general frigates etc. that lay off the Cape of Good Hope and Madagascar looking out for prizes, that some of the said ships took the EIM *Grantham* off Cape Falso bound for England from Madras with several passengers amongst which were Captains Martin, Vincent and Legg, late Captain of the fleet here. The above ships are said to be making all the preparation they can in order to attack this place. In consequence all hands here are employed in altering and strengthening the fort and works, moving guns, preparing ammunition and getting everything ready for their reception.

18 JULY
The *Diligent* Schooner (Captain McClashing) sailed with an express to Admiral Pocock of the above intelligence.

8 AUGUST
The ceremony amongst the Brahminies etc. was performed by flinging the coconuts into the sea, it being full moon.

11 AUGUST
Bombay. This morning two men and a woman were hanged, one for murder the other for theft and the woman for receiving goods knowing them to be stolen.

24 SEPTEMBER
This morning all the troops were under arms to hear Mr Draper, the Company's secretary, read at the head of the troops the grant which the Mogul had confirmed to the Honourable the East India Company of the Castle of Surat and all the revenues belonging to it etc. on which there was three volleys fired by the troops with three huzzas and all the large guns fired round the fort[28].

27 SEPTEMBER
EIM *Godolphin* (Hutchinson) arrived from England ex the Downs 28 April 1759.

---

[28] The rejoicing no doubt confirmed the hopes of the troops for the 20 lakhs of rupees promised them as a reward for the capture of Surat by the Company.

3 OCTOBER

The EIM *Harcourt* (Webber) with the *Griffin* (Dethack) and the *Clinton* (Smith) arrived here having left the Downs the same time as the *Godolphin*. The passengers were Major Fraser to command the Company's troops here, Captain Nugent, Captain/Lieutenant Walsh with a new adjutant Pointon and ten cadets for the Company's service.

18 OCTOBER

A patamar arrived with news that Admirals Pocock and Stevens with seven men of war under their command attacked 11 sail of French men of war under the command of Admiral d'Aché. After a smart engagement of about $2\frac{1}{4}$ hours the French thought proper to sheer off with all the sail they could crowd. It was imagined by our Admirals that they were coming to Pondicherry but, meeting with our fleet in Pondicherry Road, obliged the French to come to an engagement which was on 10th of last September. We lost Captain Mackay who commanded one of the men of war and two Lieutenants as also Captain Gore of the marines. The whole killed in this engagement was 120 and 402 wounded. They could not ascertain the number killed and wounded of the French. However, I believe this engagement has put a stop to their intention of attacking Bombay at least for this year.

5 NOVEMBER

Bombay. Lieutenant James Wood of the RA is appointed Quartermaster to the detachment by Captain Maitland on the room of Lieutenant Daniel Sweet who resigned by an order from England and on 18th instant Robert Harris, Sergeant RA, was appointed Lieutenant Fireworker in the room of Lieutenant Harling.

MONDAY 19 NOVEMBER

A fleet of ships consisting of five large and several small ones was seen off Bombay by one of our cruisers, and as they hoisted no colours they were taken for the French fleet, on which the signal gun was fired, and immediately it was beat to arms. Bombay all in an uproar moving and scaling the guns on the works and bringing up mortars etc. and getting everything in readiness the whole night. One of our bombardiers had his leg broke in scaling the guns.

TUESDAY 20 NOVEMBER

Bombay. About 9 am the boat returned which was sent yesterday on the discovery, who informed us that they were the Portuguese fleet consisting of three men of war, two large trading ships with several small ones. On this information the men were sent to their quarters and the gates of the town were ordered to be opened. The same day Mr Price, one of the council here, sailed from hence in order to relieve Mr Spencer who was left Chief of Surat, everything being settled there.

MONDAY 26 NOVEMBER

Accounts came here that two men of war of 64 and 20 guns belonging to the French had taken Gombroon in Persia which was a settlement belonging to the EI Company where they had a factory, having landed about 500 men and ransacked the place. They took about one lakh of rupees and about two lakhs worth of copper. After which they re-embarked their men and sailed on a cruise. A lakh is 100,000 rupees or £10,500 at 30 pence per rupee. (Count L'Estaing commanded this expedition tho' on his parole of honour.)

THURSDAY 29 NOVEMBER

General Orders. The Governor has appointed Captain Thomas Daniel Black and Captain/Lieutenant Villiers Walsh his Aide-de-Camps and Lieutenant McKay of the Company's artillery to be Quartermaster. In the same orders the Commanding Officers of the King's and Company's artillery are to divide their officers to the different bastions occupied by their particular corps. The officer commanding each bastion is strictly to examine into the state of the guns, carriages, ammunition and all other necessaries belonging to the bastion under their charge and are to be answerable that everything is at all times fit for immediate service. The Quartermasters of the King's and Company's artillery are always to keep thirty rounds of ammunition ready for each gun occupied by their different Corps, as also a sufficient quantity of spare necessaries for their different bastions. The King's artillery are to occupy all the works from the lower flank of the Dock Gate Bastion to the Church Gate and the Company's artillery all the rest of the works round the town and Castle. An orderly sergeant of the King's and Company's artillery is to visit the different bastions and ramparts occupied by their corps every morning before the relieving of the guards, and to report to their proper Commanding Officers who is immediately to report if anything is found deficient to the Commanding Officer of the Garrison[29].

3 DECEMBER
A quarrel happened some time ago between Captain/Lieutenant Walsh in the Company's service and Lieutenant Chandler of the King's artillery, but as they were both in company at Maham with other gentlemen at that time, it could not be decided. A few days after the first, a second quarrel happened, and Captain/Lieutenant Sir Charles Chalmers being in company at that time put them both under arrest. As they could not agree, a General Court Martial was ordered on 4th instant on Lieutenant Chandler who was charged by Captain Walsh of behaviour unbecoming to the character of an officer and a gentleman, but in the evening the Court Martial was countermanded until further orders.

SATURDAY 8 DECEMBER
About 4 pm several large ships were seen from one of our outposts which was supposed to be the French fleet on which the signal gun was fired. It beat to arms and the gates were shut.

SUNDAY 9 DECEMBER
Mr Spencer, who was chief of Surat and relieved by Mr Price, arrived here this morning with a large convoy of gallivats and boats. The fleet that was seen yesterday proves to be our own under the command of Admiral Stevens, on which information the gates were opened and the troops ordered back to their barracks.

MONDAY 10 DECEMBER
Bombay. The *Grafton* arrived and Admiral Stevens with the *Elizabeth, Tiger* and *Newcastle* and on 12th the *Yarmouth* arrived, Admiral Pocock with the *Cumberland* and *Salisbury*. They parted with the *Weymouth* and *Sunderland* near Tellicherry with orders to join Admiral Cornish's fleet which had lately arrived on the coast from England with four men of war viz: the *Lennox* (Admiral Cornish and Captain Joslin) 74 guns, the *Duke de Acquitaine* (Captain Sir W Hewit) 64 guns, the *York* (Captain Vincent Pierce) 60 guns, and the *Falmouth* (Captain Hughes) 50 guns,

[29] These orders probably arose from a general review of the situation ordered by the new CO of the Company's troops, Major Fraser, a King's officer who had arrived on 3 October. His zeal and authoritarian ways did not go down and he was soon superceded.

with orders to remain at Tellicherry and to be ready to sail for Madras
or Bengal in case of anything material happening on either of the said
coasts. The same morning Lieutenant Chandler desired a Court of
Inquiry which was granted.

TUESDAY 11 DECEMBER
A Court of Inquiry sat at Captain Tovey's quarters this morning in
order to see if the affair depending between Walsh and Chandler could
be determined without a Court Martial – the Royal Artillery gave 4
officers and the Company's 5 which sat.

SATURDAY 15 DECEMBER
As the affair between Walsh and Chandler could not be decided by the
Court of Inquiry, a general Court Martial is ordered to sit on 17th at
Captain Tovey's quarters, he being ordered President. The Royal
Artillery to furnish five members including the President, the
Company's artillery four and the infantry four; all evidences to attend.

MONDAY 17 DECEMBER
The Court Martial being sat, the Adjutant went for Lieutenant
Chandler who enquired how many officers of the King's Artillery was
sat. When informed five, he told the Adjutant it was illegally composed
to the rules agreeable to the King's Articles of War, which according
to the eleventh article of the fifteenth section, the King's should have
been seven including the President and the Company's but six. He
therefore told the Adjutant he would not attend on so illegal a Court
Martial. On which he sent for Captain Maitland to whom he resigned
his Lieutenant's commission, giving his reason why he did so, on
which the General Court Martial was dissolved.

29 DECEMBER
Bombay. The officers appointed to the care of the bastions, curtains
etc. are to take some men with them and see that the guns of the
bastion are properly placed in their embrasures and that the stores are
conveniently stored away in the sheds of the said bastions and the
Commanding Officers of the different bastions are to make a demand
to the storekeeper for what stores they want to complete them and to
apply to Captain Tovey for the keys of the powder chests, from whence
the old powder is to be removed and returned to the stores.

31 DECEMBER

The troops were under arms and fired three rounds, as likewise all the cannon round the island and forts on account of the Mogul's granting to the company the Castle of Surat for ever and also several other advantages of Surat which they say is worth to the company 70,000 rupees per annum. The same day we heard that Admiral Cornish had left Tellicherry on 21st in order to proceed for Madras.

5 JANUARY 1760

Marched from here the Royal Artillery under the command of Captain Tovey, Captain/Lieutenant Sir Francis Chalmers, Captain/Lieutenant Lewis, Lieutenant Hetzler, Francis Wood, Mr Plenderleath and Mr Banks, surgeon, for Byculla to practice with guns and mortars. Left only a barrack guard to do duty until their return.

10 JANUARY

Bombay. Sailed for Persia Captain Forbes, Lieutenant Hutchins and Ensign Nack with a command of 80 men and Lieutenant Peppard, with 1 sergeant, 1 bombardier, 4 gunners and 6 mattrosses for Gambroon in order to settle the English factory which the French had lately demolished.

21 JANUARY

Captain Winter, Captain/Lieutenant Barrett marched this morning with Lieutenants Sweet, Scott, Brereton, Davis, Moffatt, Harris and Doctor Vans to relieve the other officers at Byculla.

25 JANUARY

A Board of Officers of the King's Artillery to be held at Captain Tovey's quarters, he being president, to consist of nine, to sit at 10 am tomorrow to enquire whether the late General Court Martial intended for the trial of Lieutenant Chandler charged by Captain Walsh was legally composed to rule agreeable to the articles of war. The paymaster to pay the Royal Artillery their arrears for the last year, and all the officers both civil and military of the Royal Artillery to meet at Captain Maitland's quarters tomorrow at 8 am.

MONDAY 4 FEBRUARY

Bombay. The King's Artillery marched into quarters from the practice at Byculla and mounted a barrack guard.

Tuesday 5 February

Orders by Major Fraser: A captain in the Company's service to take charge of the main guard, and all the guards for the future are ordered to march off at 8 am, the whole to parade together on the Grand Parade; all beating to begin from the main guard, the troop to beat at sunrise, retreat at sunset and tattoo at 9 pm, after which no soldier off duty is to be seen out of their quarters. Captain Heany of the Company's infantry who was tried by a general court martial is acquitted of the charge laid against him. The Governor and council have thought proper to dismiss Lieutenant Peter Cockey of the Company's service for general bad behaviour and in consequence of a certificate signed by the officers doing duty in Surat garrison charging him with some very scandalous and infamous practices. This morning the Royal Artillery mounted the castle guard which consisted of two Lieutenants, 2 sergeants, 2 corporals, 4 bombardiers, drummer and fifer, with 26 gunners and mattrosses on account of the Company's artillery going to the practice of the gun and mortar at Byculla. The officer of the Castle guard to make his reports, one to Captain Maitland and another to the Captain of the main guard: the youngest officer on that guard to see the roll calls of the Royal Artillery in the Castle as usual and to make his report to Captain Maitland. The same evening a patamar arrived from Madras with an account of an engagement between the English commanded by Colonel Coote and the French commanded by General Lally and that our troops had taken from the French two places called Wandewash and Calmscooly or Carangooly, in which places they took 45 pieces of cannon, a great quantity of ammunition, and 800 or 900 prisoners, in December 1759[30]. The English lost near 200 with several officers. The French lost by their own account about the same number. It is expected that a general engagement cannot be avoided, as both the armies are encamped within sight of each other. We have there Colonel Coote's and Draper's regiments with Captain Hislop's company of Royal Artillery besides the company's troops. The whole is reckoned to be about 3000 Europeans, and it is hoped that Admiral Cornish will be there in time with his six ships that left Tellicherry on 21 December. We hear that General Lally has about the same number of Europeans. It is thought the fate of India very much depends on the success of this battle. The same patamar also brought a pacquet to Admiral Pocock of an engagement between the English

---

[30] Colonel Eyre Coote took over from Major Brereton (79th Foot (Draper's)) on 21 November.

and Dutch on the coast of Bengal. It seems the Dutch sent four large ships and 3 others with 1400 troops under the command of Colonel Rupel which arrived in the river Hooghly in October 1759 for Chinchura, but Colonel Clive would not allow them to pass up the river nor their landing; on which they took several of the company's trading vessels, and were for forcing their way into the river and landing their people, on which Colonel Clive sent 3 EI ships to engage them, viz: the *Duke of Dorset*, *Hardwick* and *Calcutta*, and Colonel Forde to attack them by land. After a severe fire on both sides between the ships the Commodore of the Dutch at last struck his flag, on which Captain Wilson took possession of the four Dutch ships – the other two got off, and the other seen aground. On 25 November Colonel Forde attacked them by land and totally routed them. 300 of the prisoners taken at Calcutta entered into the EI company's service and the rest were sent back to the Dutch, agreeable to the proposals of accommodation being sent to Colonel Clive by the Directors and Council of the Dutch factory at Chinchura which was concluded on 1 December 1759. Captain/Lieutenant Campbell of the Royal Artillery died of the wound he received in his thigh at the Battle of Wandewash.

SATURDAY 9 FEBRUARY

Bombay. This morning the *Dragon* (Captain Attenborough) sailed for Surat with Councillor Ellis and Commodore James of the Company's marines as passengers. They intend going overland from Surat to Europe. The same day a quarrel happened between Commissary Chandler and Conductor Vans both of HM Artillery, on account of some disagreeable words which passed between them when he went to muster the RA at Byculla at the beginning of this month. When Mr Vans came from Byculla Mr Chandler demanded satisfaction for the abuse he said he had received at Byculla, on which Vans told him that when he had cleared his character with Captain Walsh, he would then give him what satisfaction he demanded. Until then he did not think himself on a footing with him. Therefore it passed over until this day, when Chandler called on him again and was informed he was at a sale of goods at Captain Hough's. Chandler waited his coming out, went up and told him he demanded satisfaction and desired Vans immediately to draw, on which they both drew, made some pushes at each other (but before anybody came up to part them, though in the middle of the day and on the open green) Chandler gave Vans a wound in his right breast which was so deep that it pierced his lungs, at which Vans dropped, and Chandler made his escape to the waterside, got a boat and sailed to the other side and got to the island of Salsett amongst the Mahrattas before anybody could tell what was become of him. Guards were immediately despatched all round the island of Bombay in pursuit of him, and a guard and sentries planted around his house. Orders were sent to the outposts to examine all boats passing and going to the other side. Mr Vans in the meanwhile was carried home and a consultation of doctors called, which were of the general opinion that he could not live until the next day as the wound bled inwardly very much, and also coming out of his mouth, but Mr Lyne came in and ordered him to be bled immediately. He probed and dressed his wound and put him to rest; the next day he was much better and they are in hopes of his recovery.

17 FEBRUARY
Captain Maitland has appointed Sergeant James Crooks Lieutenant Fireworker in the room of Lieutenant Chandler resigned.

20 FEBRUARY
Bombay. A quarrel happened between Captain Tovey and Captain/Lieutenant Barrett (both of the RA) on one of the bastions which occasioned them to draw, and after making a few passes at each other Captain Barrett ran Captain Tovey in the sword arm a little above his wrist, which wound occasioned him to drop his sword, on which the affair was settled, and as it was not a wound of any great consequence no further notice was taken.

27 FEBRUARY
All the troops in the garrison were ordered under arms to receive Governor Bourchier on his going aboard the *Clinton* EIM (Captain Smith) bound for Europe. As he passed, the officers saluted, and the men rested their arms, and likewise did the same to Mr Crommelin, who succeeds Mr Bourchier in the Government here. The men of war were likewise manned and gave three cheers on his embarkation and 17 guns fired from HMS *Yarmouth*, Admiral Pocock's ship, and all the company's ships saluted as he passed. The Admiral sent HMS *Elizabeth* (Captain Dent) of 50 guns to convoy him as far as Tellicherry. He passed by the fort about 6 pm.

29 FEBRUARY
Bombay. This morning three of the black people were found murdered; two with their heads cut off, and the other at a little distance from them with his throat cut.

1 MARCH

Bombay. An anonymous letter direct to Captain Hough dated 29 February was found this morning informing him that it was his fault that the gratuity money of Surat was not paid, and if he did not give a sufficient reason before 7 April he might expect his house to be levelled to the ground, informing him at the same time that they carried 13 rounds of powder and ball with scaling ladders, ropes etc. The Governor, Major Fraser, Captain Maitland and Mr Hough have offered 100 rupees each to any person or persons who shall discover anyone concerned therein with a promise of pardon besides the reward, to any who shall discover his or their accomplices.

The same evening a patamar arrived from Madras with the joyful news that the English had defeated the French under the command of General Lally on 21 January 1760, the English under the command of Colonel Coote. It is said the French had 2100 Europeans, 300 cofferees, 8000 sepoys besides cavalry and 25 pieces of cannon; the English had 1700 Europeans including cavalry, 3000 sepoys, 14 pieces of cannon and one howitzer. After a smart engagement for two or three hours the whole French line gave way and fled under cover of their own cannon imagining we should pursue them. They had about 800 men killed and wounded, General Bussy being taken prisoner; the English lost in the field 86 killed and about 150 wounded: amongst the former was Major Brereton. We took in the field 22 pieces of cannon and great quantity of their baggage. On the success of this battle the English laid siege to Chittapet and took the whole garrison prisoners of war and took the Chevalier De Tilley. Timery was reduced. From thence they went to Arcot, the capital of that province, laid siege and took it in a few days in which were 200 Europeans and 300 sepoys, 20 pieces of cannon and 4 mortars so that the English are now masters of the Cormandel coast, and the French troops have nothing to take care of but their own garrison at Pondicherry which they are putting in the best order they can. On the information of the above news which arrived at 6.30 pm, a Royal Salute of 21 pieces of cannon was fired from the fort[31].

---

[31] The figures of strength and losses are remarkably accurate. Because Lally was besieging Wandewash at the time, he did not deploy his full strength against Coote. The battle opened the way to operations against Pondicherry itself. English artillery was very effective.

2 MARCH

Bombay. News arrived to Admiral Pocock from Bengal that the English, Dutch and the Nabob of Bengal, had almost compromised matters relative to the late affair on that coast, and that the Dutch are willing to make any restitution, having acknowledged themselves the aggressors etc.

MONDAY 3 MARCH

Bombay. This morning all the troops in the garrison were under arms, when the Secretary, Mr Draper, at the head of the troops read Mr Crommelin's commission, appointing him (by the Honourable Court of Directors) Governor etc of the Island and Castle of Bombay on which the troops fired three rounds and gave three cheers, and the Castle fired 21 guns and likewise the outforts fired all their cannon, after which the officers went and paid their compliments to the Governor at his house.

13 MARCH

All the Company's infantry marched from hence for Byculla this morning to learn the gun and mortar exercise, as likewise the method of encamping. The guard for Bombay ordered from the camp every two days, the Royal Artillery to take charge of all the works in the Castle and the Company's artillery to take charge of all the bastions and curtains round the ramparts.

FRIDAY 14 MARCH

Bombay. This morning Admiral Stevens sailed from hence in the *Grafton*, with HMS *Tiger* and *Elizabeth* and the *Revenge*, a 20-gun ship belonging to the Company commanded by Commodore Watson.

THURSDAY 3 APRIL

120,000 rupees was delivered amongst the troops as gratuity money for taking the Castle and works of Surat; when shared these came to Captain Maitland as commanding the marine 3560, to each of the captains 1004, to Lieutenants 902, to NCO's 136, to private men 24, to sepoys 16 rupees each.

SUNDAY 6 APRIL

Bombay. This afternoon Admiral Pocock embarked on board the *Yarmouth* (Captain Harrison) in order to sail for England. The company of Grenadiers were ordered from Byculla camp to receive

him as he went on board and about 2 the next evening the *Yarmouth*
was under sail and was saluted by the fort and also by the Company's
ships, which was returned from the *Yarmouth* with 17 guns to the fort
and 15 to the Company's ships.

SATURDAY 12 APRIL
Bombay. The weather being so excessive hot the Company was obliged
to break up their camp at Byculla and marched to their quarters here.

MONDAY 14 APRIL
Captain Heany's company of infantry embarked with Captain Nugent's
company of Grenadiers and Captain/Lieutenant Nielsen, Lieutenant
Cranson and Lieutenant Wilder with 26 privates of the Company's
artillery, on an expedition to assist the Sidees against the Mahrattas
and Portuguese who have laid siege to Rogepore, a port belonging to
the Sidees.

TUESDAY 15 APRIL
Bombay. The *Bombay* grab (Captain Kable) with the *Guardian* (Captain
Good) and the *Griffin* Indiaman (Captain Dethack) as also the *Success*
and *Viper* bomb ketches, sailed this evening with the command that
embarked yesterday for Fort Rogepore or rather Fort Gingerly.

MONDAY 21 APRIL
The command that embarked last Monday returned this evening and
brought account that the fleet belonging to the Portuguese and
Mahrattas saluted our ships and sailed off with their forces, without
any more trouble.

SATURDAY 3 MAY
A patamar arrived from Madras to Bombay reporting the want of land
forces, both artillery and infantry, as Colonel Coote intended to lay
siege to Pondicherry, the chief settlement of the French on the
Coromandel coast, he having great success in taking most of their
small settlements in the East Indies.

INDIA – THE FINAL PHASE
MAY 1760–JUNE 1765

At this point the original manuscript diary ends and the second volume is missing. Luckily Colonel Laws made a summary typescript. This concentrates on the detail most likely to interest a gunner. However, the entries are less frequent and I feel it is sufficient to round off Wood's story with a final narrative section.

Leaving Bombay on 4 May 1760 with Captain Maitland's company aboard H M S *Salisbury* (50 guns) James Wood disembarked at Cuddalore on 26 May to find Major Monson and Colonel Eyre Coote (late 39th) in mid-campaign attacking a number of French posts in succession, knocking away the props, as it were, to their coastal fortress base of Pondicherry. In particular their aim was to isolate the town from the parts of the Deccan and Mysore whence Bussy had long drawn supplies and men.

On their landing, Coote at once sent by messenger for the three reinforcing companies of Royal Artillery from Bombay to join him in camp outside Valdore some 9 miles from Pondicherry. About 4 miles from camp he personally greeted them on the road and the following day all the R A officers enjoyed his hospitality at dinner. Coote also had with him Captain Barker and his company of Madras artillery.

In the middle of June the British troops were much cheered at the news of Wolfe's triumph at Quebec and of Admiral Hawke's great victory in Quiberon Bay in November 1759. James Wood now saw action with the artillery against Villanore. This place fell on July 20 and Wood records that one of his colleagues, Lieutenant Plenderleith, was wounded.

Further infantry reinforcements having now arrived from England at Cuddalore in a convoy of eleven East Indiamen, operations for the final investment and capture of Pondicherry were set on. First a mobile column of "Hussar" native cavalry under Captain de Beck, with two field guns R A under Lieutenant Harris, was led by Coote to intercept a party of Mysorean horse trying to bring in cattle on the hoof for the French commissariat. The Mysoreans were soundly defeated and the cattle rounded up for British use.

In addition to Coote's own 84th Regiment, Draper's 79th, fresh from home, were now in the field. Early in September Colonel Stanley Morris's 89th Regiment of Highlanders moved up from Cuddalore under command of the famous Major Hector Monro. Over 600 sepoys together with a number of topasses completed the besieging force. Although a French counterattack on the Royal Artillery holding the captured fort at Tamarind Tope succeeded in capturing a short 6-pounder and taking prisoner Lieutenant Sanders R A and three gunners, the *point d'appui* held out. Wood also reports the supercession of Coote in command by Monson when the latter suddenly received a promotion from the E I Directors in London by letter in September. Coote was certainly put out but all was soon forgotten when Monson was wounded in the attack on the Bound Hedge battery and asked for Coote to return and take over. "We drove the French out but with little advantage," writes Wood of this action, having 36 men killed and 70 wounded including Lieutenant Davies R A fighting in and around the Bound Hedge lines for nearly three weeks. After the French had blown up the Arescopang redoubt they retook the Madras redoubt of the Bound Hedge on 2 October and held it. There was evidently considerable artillery activity to batter down the line of fortifications on the landward side. The Madras redoubt was twice taken and retaken, according to Wood, who particularly mourned the loss of a promising young engineer officer Ensign McMahon of Draper's. By 13 October Coote was sufficiently confident and merciful to allow the French to send out from the beleaguered garrison the "*bouches inutiles*" of their womenfolk. The marked absence of French naval support made surrender but a matter of time. During January there was further bitter fighting around St Thomas redoubt which was taken and then retaken in a night attack. Lieutenant Collins R A and seven gunners were captured only to be returned next morning by the storming French. This was the last throw. On 10 January Lally put out the white flag. Unfortunately Coote's A D C Lieutenant de Webb was mistakenly shot through with a cannon ball when going forward to meet the flag of truce. On 15 January the terms of the capitulation for Pondicherry were agreed.

It is of note that Wood records that so close were the working relations of the Royal and Company artillery companies at Pondicherry that Coote appointed Captain Barker, Madras Artillery, to be Major of Brigade to the whole artillery contingent in his force. The French were clearly in low morale after so long a siege, and quarrelsome. Their

Commissary General lost his life in "a sort of duel", reported Wood. "Not a cat, dog or rat was to be seen, all having been eaten". In keeping with the rest of the Diary Wood strikes few personal notes. To the 18th century soldier everything seems to have been accepted as normal, no question of wanting life to be arranged otherwise and so little ground for comment, grumble or speculation. The daily round and common task were enough for that philosophy now moulded by several years of experience in the Orient, with the sharper emphasis between life and death which man could do little to modify. It is no good looking for signs of 20th century attitudes in a plain man's diary of the mid-18th century. It is indeed difficult for the modern reader to understand the total absence of sentimentality in that harsh age.

Colonel Draper's Regiment took exception to the fact that Coote sent in his own grenadier company to get the first pickings in Pondicherry but were satisfied that Coote could justify his action by the longer service in India of his regiment though in precedence it was junior. Captain Hislop, the senior officer of the R A Company in Madras, went off to Madras to settle his affairs in the middle of the long siege and came back with orders from the King that the Royal Artillery were to take in no more volunteers. Since this was the way that Wood had started he was no doubt somewhat mystified. He noted that local recruitment of officers to the Royal Artillery was carried forward by other means; Francis Keith of Morris's Highlanders transferred as Lieutenant Fireworker; Mr Peter Duff came from being a volunteer in the 89th and two plain "gentlemen", Mr James Burnett and Mr James Capes, came in from civilian life. Soon after the fall of Pondicherry the Royal Artillery in the Madras Presidency was reorganized so as to provide a company under Captain Winter to go to Manila in Draper's force, aboard the fleet of Admiral Cornish. The companies of Captain Maitland, Captain Barrett and Captain Phoenix, with Wood in the first named, embarked at Pondicherry for Bombay, all supernumeraries temporarily attached to the Royal Artillery being returned to their infantry regiments. En route it was learnt that Major Monro and his Highlanders had captured Mahé on the Malabar shore and were moving further inland. Captain Barrett's company R A sent one officer and twelve gunners to strengthen Captain Nielsen's company of Bombay artillery in Munro's column. Royal and Company artillery now worked almost as a single Regiment. Early in April, 1761, Wood was delighted to be back in Bombay, being sent to new quarters for the Royal Artillery at Sion outside the town. In June he was promoted First Lieutenant, thanks to the unusual occurrence of an officer senior to him being sent home on promotion: Captain/Lieutenant Whitmore.

As soon as Draper's expedition left Madras for Manila two infantry companies from Monson's 96th Regiment and three officers and fifty men from the Company's Artillery left Bombay to replace them. In November, 1762, Maitland heard that he had been promoted to Major, with effect from the previous March in recognition of his having commanded the Royal Artillery in India since the departure of Wood's original patron, John Chalmers, in 1759. Maitland only survived until 21 February, 1763, when he was buried with fitting ceremony, James Wood taking a leading part in the obsequies as a Captain/Lieutenant. The whole council of the Bombay Presidency turned out and the saluting battery on the Castle fired 60 half-minute guns. Three short 6-pounders were drawn by the artillery behind the firing party of officers, the middle gun "draped with the Union Flag in mourning". The Royal and Bombay artillery united in tribute.

Early in 1763 a mixed East India Company force left Bombay for the Gulf to move the factory from Gambroon (Bandar Abbas) to Basra and to set up a new factory at Bushire in the face of some Persian resistance.

May, 1763, found the Madras Presidency fearful of French raids and to their cry for help Colonel Morris, now senior King's officer at Bombay, decided to despatch James Wood with four other officers and 56 gunners to strengthen the defences of the Carnatic base area. It was not long before James Wood found himself once more marching to the support of Colonel Monson in the field at Vellore. However, a few days later news of the Peace of Paris reached the Governor of Madras, and Captain Winter, senior R A officer, was ordered to embark for England with all stores and men. Before they could be got ready further instructions arrived from King George III to say that officers and N C Os could transfer to the East India Company army on the same terms held out to the 39th in 1757: the offer was of 10 pagodas [35 rupees] a man for a 3-year contract. Wood notes only that Lieutenants Duff and Chandler accepted. On 9 November, 1763, Lieutenants James Wood, Hetzler, Plenderleith (recovered of his wound), Brereton and Keith embarked for home on H M S *Weymouth*, 60 guns, Captain Collins R N. After battling against terrific storms Collins had to put into Bombay for repairs. In the process he received orders to return to Madras because of great alarm in the Bay of Bengal. Sailing as soon as he could, taking with him the unfortunate Wood and Hetzler, he made once more for Madras. It was a false alarm and by now Draper's men had returned from Manila, their prize money withheld. Those of Winter's company who did not choose to stay on with the Company joined with Hetzler and Wood and all set sail finally for England: a party of about

30 gunners, all that remained of the original five companies that had been despatched to India since 1755, including those aboard the ill-fated *Dodington*.

Reaching the Cape in December they met Lord Clive outward bound on his last tour aboard E I M *Kent*. After two months at the Cape, Wood touches at St Helena where he meets up with Captain Barrett and two invalids R A. He hears news that Major Winter and four of the officers from the Manila/Madras party had sailed home ahead of him.

On 21 June, 1765, Wood reaches Plymouth after touching at Kinsale. He had been away from England over ten years since sailing from the Thames in March, 1755. For the voyages after his first arrival in Bombay he kept no notes on distances travelled or states of wind and tide, and gives us only the barest information on the main stages of his long journey home. Life subjected so continuously over so long a period to the exigencies of "a maritime strategy" had become a little tedious perhaps to a professional gunner. After twenty years of movement about the world, his horizons were now to be limited to Colchester, Portsmouth and Woolwich until final retirement and death in 1797.

INDEX

INDEX